Unintended Consequences:

How to Improve our Government, our Businesses, and our Lives

Also by Harlan Platt

Business Books

Why Companies Fail: Strategies for Detecting, Avoiding and Profiting from Bankruptcy

The First Junk Bond: A Story of Corporate Boom and Bust

Principles of Corporate Renewal

The Phoenix Effect: 9 Revitalizing Strategies No Business Can Do Without (with Carter Pate)

Chipping: The New Stock Market Method for Surviving Turbulence and Hitting a Hole-in-One

A Case Book on Corporate Renewal (with Marjorie Platt)

Counterintuitive Investing

Lead with Cash

Other Books

One Plus One

Unintended Consequences:
How to Improve our Government, our Businesses, and our Lives

Harlan D. Platt

Charles L Webster Publishers

For my grandchildren who are not unintended consequences

Table of Contents

Chapter 1

Introduction to Unintended Consequences

Unintended consequences are unavoidable. They materialize whether we want them to or not. Sometimes, they are beneficial; more often than not, they are harmful. The inevitability of unintended consequences is like a natural phenomenon, but unlike nature, unintended consequences can often be controlled. This book explains how society can control some unintended consequences so as to minimize their impacts. Some might ask, "if sometimes unintended consequences yield positive effects, why control them?" The answer is that we don't know which unintended consequences will be positive and the damage inflicted by negative unintended consequences, that might have been controlled, may be enormous. Depending on chance is not a good strategy; that is why we look before crossing the street. Not controlling unintended consequences, when they can be, is reckless. This book proposes a more defensive approach to unintended consequences.

Unintended consequences are like a roll of dice in a Las Vegas casino. Until the dice bounce off the bumpers it is unclear how many points they will show; similarly what unintended consequences will do and who they will affect may be unclear for years or even decades. Taking chances on the outcome of events rather than considering how they might affect the future is a bad decision. Society needs to limit the unintended consequences that it can control.

Before proceeding, let me describe what I mean by an unintended consequence. Do you remember the scene at the beginning of the movie the *Wizard of Oz* when the little dog Toto bites Miss Gulch and Dorothy leaves home to try and save her pet? Arriving back home with Toto after the rescue, Dorothy is by herself when the tornado strikes and she gets hit on the head and knocked out by a flying window. Dorothy then wakes up in the Land of Oz. Toto's actions, biting the evil Miss Gulch, led to the unintended consequence of Dorothy being transported to the Land of Oz.

Without the plot device of an unintended consequence one of the greatest books and movies would have had a hard time explaining how a little girl from Kansas got to Oz. But the *Wizard of Oz* is fiction and like all fiction its author had the power to control his characters' destiny. Life is not so providential nor is it so nicely scripted. Problems we encounter because of unintended consequences don't mysteriously disappear with a click of our heels.

Unintended consequences are sometimes beneficial. Consider the discovery of penicillin in 1928 by Alexander Fleming. As the legend is told, Dr. Fleming accidentally left uncovered a petri dish containing Staphylococcus bacteria. When he returned the next morning, a mold had taken root in the petri dish and around that mold the growth of the Staphylococcus bacteria was inhibited. By refining the mold Fleming created penicillin. Since his discovery, penicillin and other antibiotics that followed it have saved the lives and limbs of millions of human beings. Penicillin derives from an unintended consequence, a positive unintended consequence caused by Dr. Fleming's forgetfulness. Obviously, efforts to control unintended consequences need to allow other Dr. Flemings to make scientific breakthroughs.

A simple example of a negative unintended consequence, to balance the positive outcome in the Dr. Fleming story, took place in the Florida Everglades. Over the years, countless parents who had purchased Burmese pythons as pets for their children released the reptiles into the wild or flushed them down their toilets after discovering that pythons grow rather large. The freed pythons were fruitful and their offspring have devoured the Everglades' fauna including birds, deer and even alligators. The region's ecology has changed. Certainly none of these individuals envisioned the eventual damage their actions would cause. But that is the problem with unintended consequences – they occur whether or not we anticipate their impact.

The cumulative impact of unintended consequences, trading off the good against the bad, is incalculable. We don't even know which are more likely: positive or negative unintended consequences. What is known is that unintended consequences arise when and where they are not expected, they affect the agent whose action created them as well as others and they may be more consequential than the original action which caused them. Readers versed in economics might be wondering whether I am talking about externalities. The answer is both yes and no because externalities are a type of unintended consequence; however, not all unintended consequences are externalities. A comparison between externalities and unintended consequences is available in the final chapter.

Unintended consequences are not on most people's radar screen. The patient in a hospital whose life is saved by penicillin is unlikely to remark, "Thank you Dr. Fleming." Likewise, a patient who becomes seriously ill because they are allergic to penicillin is unlikely to say, "I wish Dr. Fleming had covered that petri dish." For the most part people are unaware of how their lives, happiness, and fortune are influenced by the actions of others through the power and omnipresence of unintended consequences.

Our society contains billions of individuals each of whom makes countless decisions every day. Each of those decisions produces wave upon wave of unintended consequences. By secluding ourselves in a locked room and by doing the exact same thing every day, we can reduce the number of unintended consequences that affect us. But that is an impractical solution. We need to go outside in order to work and to interact with others. This book discusses how some types of unintended consequences can be contained and controlled. If its dictums are followed unintended consequences will not vanish but their severity and frequency will be reduced. We will never live in a world free of unintended consequences. However, it is possible to control the biggest perpetrator of the most damaging unintended consequences, the ones that inflict the most harm on innocent victims.

Each chapter in this book presents a number of unintended consequences caused by a specific agent. Chapter 2 contains unintended consequences that arise from government decision-making. It is the longest chapter in the book because the government makes so many decisions with negative unintended consequences. Some might argue that documenting governmental unintended consequences is like shooting ducks in a barrel; others might contend that the exercise is unfair because the government is required to make laws and promulgate regulations. Both arguments are invalid: the first because most people are unfamiliar with the government's role in creating negative unintended consequences, the second argument because there is a division between those things that the government must do to protect and improve the lives of its citizens and those things that a government wants to do for a variety of reasons. This important distinction is less about the lines that can be drawn between political philosophies or parties and more about governments that create legislation in areas known or expected to harbor quicksand, i.e. unintended consequences. Some of these decisions should not be included in government's realm and should instead be left to individual decision-making.

The third chapter catalogs unintended consequences inspired by human behavior. Science related unintended consequences are presented in Chapter 4. Technologically driven unintended consequences are in Chapter 5. Chapter 6 presents corporate unintended consequences. Unintended consequences in the medical arena are given their own space in Chapter 7. The final chapter compares unintended consequences to externalities.

The selection of the appropriate chapter for each unintended consequence was not easy. Many unintended consequences spanned several chapters and could have been placed in either. When this ambiguity is possibly distracting I have indicated where else the unintended consequence could have gone.

Unintended consequences are interesting but a book about interesting things might not itself be interesting. While I hope the book is enjoyable, I have written it so that others learn that unintended consequences can cause greater harm than the good created by the initial action itself. The last chapter which is more academic in tone than the rest of the book carefully explains the differences between externalities and unintended consequences. It also discusses how the total cost of unintended consequences vary depending on whether they derive from human, corporate, or governmental decisions. Human decisions mostly affect the small group of people associated with the decision-maker and so even when a human decision causes an unintended consequence the aggregate impact is generally small. Hence, there is little reason and limited ability to control human-based unintended consequences. Corporate decisions, especially in a world that is rapidly globalizing, have a wider scope than do individual human decisions and consequently the aggregate impact of unintended consequences coming from companies is greater than those caused by people. Efforts to limit corporate unintended consequences before they occur by creating further regulations of companies are shortsighted; the controls are likely to inhibit corporate innovation, entrepreneurship, and ultimately economic growth and prosperity. Controlling corporate related unintended consequences therefore doesn't make sense either.

The remaining agent causing unintended consequences is the government. Governmental decisions affect almost everybody and their unintended consequences impact people worldwide. There are few restraints on government limiting which laws they can enact. What is needed is the enactment of a "do-no-harm rule" to restrain governmental bodies large and small and require them to assess proposed regulations and legislation for possible unintended consequences. With the do-no-harm-rule no law could be enacted until the governmental body certified that after careful analysis it did not expect negative unintended consequences that might outweigh the legislations benefits.

No one has a crystal ball and the commission of errors is human. Even after the passage of a do-no-harm rule unintended consequences will still arise from governmental actions. What the law will do is to reduce the number and severity of governmental-based unintended consequences.

Realistically a do-no-harm rule is unlikely to be implemented in the near future. My hope is that influential decision-makers will read this book and agree with its thesis: that unintended consequences are both harmful and beneficial, that those caused by humans and companies are less harmful than those caused by the government, and that governmental unintended consequences can be limited by forcing government to reflect upon the possible unintended consequences of its decisions. If that is accomplished, then this book will have succeeded.

Chapter 2

Governmental Unintended Consequences

Governmental unintended consequences are common and generally harmful. Examples are presented in this chapter. As you read them consider the horror experienced in high school when a lunch tray is dropped. The next sound that is heard is the cheering of classmates as they celebrate someone else's misfortune. A similar transference is experienced on highways when speeding drivers slow down to participate in a gaper's block; they are willing to drive below the legal speed limit to bear witness to someone else's misfortune. While reading about governmental unintended consequences, resist the urge to cheer or gawk at the side of the road and instead use the examples to learn about and understand the dangers of governmental actions that have failed to pass a "do-no-harm rule."

There are two critical questions about governmental unintended consequences: 1. Was inaction a reasonable alternative at the time? 2. Did the government's actions lead to a better, safer, cleaner, or otherwise improved world? In far too many cases the answers to both questions are no. The reason for negative responses to the first question, nothing should have been done, is that emotions run high, often stirred up by special interest groups, so that "doing something and not just sitting here" becomes the catchword in legislative halls. Politicians mistakenly believe that they have been sent to the legislature to pass laws and so when something happens they believe it is their duty that they pass a law to somehow control, limit, regulate, or outlaw it. For example, in August 2011 when considering how to create jobs after many failed government attempts, Representative Sander Levin of Michigan said "there needs to be action." [1] He didn't ask "why after over two years of trying have all of our previous efforts failed?" Instead, he advocated taking action. The belief that the government can solve all problems is generally mistaken.

Rarely if ever does one hear about a legislature debating whether their actions might bring more harm than the event they are trying to control. Instead, armed with little or no information and a righteous purpose they enact legislation which they or a special interest group hope is in the best interest of everyone. By passing a do-no-harm rule legislative bodies would be required to take a deep breath and consider the likelihood that what they are proposing might bring more harm than good.

The second question "did the government's actions lead to a better, safer cleaner or otherwise improved world?"

---

[1] Kristina Peterson, "White House Renews Push to Extend Payroll-Tax Cut," *The Wall Street Journal*, August 6-7, 2011.

will often have a negative answer too because damaging unintended consequences arise so often. In Plato's, *The Republic,* he talks about shadows hitting the wall of a cave in which some people have lived for their entire lives chained to the ground. All these captives have ever seen of the outside world are shadows projected into the cave by people, animals and objects moving in front of a fire located outside of the cave. With this allegory Plato argued that what people think of as reality is in fact distorted[2]. Virulent unintended consequences arise from governmental actions in part because legislators, like the prisoners chained up in Plato's cave, do not always have a clear sense of reality.

A great example of a distorted sense of reality was the passage by the US Congress on August 7, 1964 of the Gulf of Tonkin resolution. It enabled President Johnson to assist any country in Southeast Asia thought to be at risk from communist aggression. Three days prior to the passage of this resolution US forces appeared to have been attacked for a <u>second</u> time (the first attack took place on August 2) by North Vietnamese naval forces. US forces responded with heavy fire for over two hours and the navy initially claimed that it had sunk two North Vietnamese torpedo boats. The task force commander, Captain John J Herrick, within hours of the initial communiqué to Washington reported that he was now doubtful that an attack had taken place and he consoled a thorough evaluation before taking further action. Nonetheless, President Johnson broadcast to the nation his determination to respond militarily; Congress passed the resolution forthwith. Recently, it has come to light that the second attack which served as sufficient pretext for the US to militarily engage the North Vietnamese was probably fictional. Even President Johnson expressed doubt in 1965 about the incident when he described the torpedo boats as possibly being whales. In 2005, a historian for the US National Security Agency (NSA) concluded that the NSA had

---

[2] He further argued that the philosopher perceives the true reality

11

distorted the report it passed on to legislators in an effort to cover up honest yet inaccurate intelligence errors. [3]

We think we know what we know but often find that we don't know anything. We are told things by people who claim to be 100% certain only to discover that they were 100% wrong. It is simply impossible for a legislative body to achieve a fair and balanced legislative solution to an apparent problem in a world in which information is easily distorted and hidden, special interests pursue an agenda of their own, and fleeting shadows flit across the walls of our room.

The noted sociologist, Robert K Merton, summed up the inability of policy makers to improve society saying that their "paramount concern with the foreseen immediate consequences excludes the consideration of further or other consequences."[4] Merton understood how politicians suffer from a myopia that enables them to only see what is happening today. Bringing relief to today's problems is all that matters even if the result of such relief is the creation of future problems which conceivably exceed in scope or scale the original problem. The condition is not confined to American government but is endemic to the species. Having a House of Representatives reelected on a two year cycle is no more the cause of political shortsightedness than is the fact that politicians meet with constituents and face superficial inquiries that are concerned only with knowing when an immediate solution will be forthcoming. The question faced is "when will you do something" rather than "what should be done?"

That is not to say that there is no need for an intelligent and thoughtful government. There are many

---

[3] Scott Shane, 2005,"Vietnam War Intelligence 'Deliberately Skewed,' Secret Study Says," *The New York Times*, December 2.
[4] Quoted in an article by Karl Rove, "The Bad News about ObamaCare Keeps Piling Up," *The Wall Street Journal*, June 17 2010.

issues that must be examined and legislated by government. The arguments above contend that an unfettered and uncontrolled government is as likely to miss the target when it passes legislation as it is to hit the target. When the damage caused by unintended consequences are factored into the equation the balance would seem to swing against an activist government trying to remedy and placate all of the economic, social, psychological, and environmental concerns of a modern society. When the government decides to act, issues should be examined within the context of the do-no-harm rule.

Special interest groups manipulate events to serve their own purpose. A worthy example is Teddy Roosevelt and the war in Cuba in 1898 (referred to as The Spanish-American War). In the prior year, President McKinley had appointed Roosevelt to be the Assistant Secretary of the navy (circumstances allowed Roosevelt to act as the de facto Secretary much of the time). Roosevelt fervently hoped the US would go to war. At one point he said, "I should welcome almost any war, for I think this country needs one."[5] Meanwhile, a newspaper owner, William Randolph Hearst, was looking for a sensational story to help him sell newspapers. He said "you furnish the pictures, and I'll furnish the war." The mysterious sinking in Cuba in February 1898 of the *USS Maine* and the unfortunate death of over 200 US sailors was exploited by Hearst to stir up jingoist feelings. The US soon declared war against Spain, the colonial power controlling Cuba. Roosevelt quickly resigned from government and took command of a volunteer army corps known as the Roughriders. Evan Thomas wrote in *The War Lovers: Roosevelt, Lodge, Hearst, and the Rush to Empire, 1898*, that Roosevelt and Hearst were not fool hardy adventures but instead were shrewd adventurers pursuing a weaker opponent. He quotes John Hay a prominent statesman at the time of describing it as a "splendid little

---

[5] *Crucible of Empire - Timeline*. PBS Online.
http://www.pbs.org/crucible/Transcript.txt.

war" that America would surely win. [6] The quick victory 10 weeks later benefited Roosevelt personally. Shortly afterward he ran for and won the Governorship of New York, was selected as the running mate for President McKinley in 1890, and became president less than a year later in 1891 when McKinley was assassinated. Laws passed following special interest group lobbying efforts often have dubious merit and are most in need of the do-no-harm rule.

How They Make Hotdogs

One of the deepest and longest lasting economic downturns in US history began December 2007 and "officially" ended in June 2009 though its effects on jobs and income lasted far longer. More is said later in this book on this topic. For the moment consider one major governmental response to the crisis. In May 2010 Congress debated a 1,500 page bill, Restoring American Financial Stability Act (RAFSA) of 2010,[7] aimed at regulating Wall Street.[8] This legislation emerged from a frustrated Congress unsure of what to do or how to act and as a consequence it has a limited likelihood of creating a safer financial system and is more likely to simply damage the institutions it is trying to improve in some way presently unknown. The unintended consequences have not emerged yet but are likely to be substantial.

---

[6] See Evan Thomas, *The War Lovers: Roosevelt, Lodge, Hearst, and the Rush to Empire, 1898,* Little, Brown & Company, Boston, 2010.

[7] Often the names given by Congress to legislation mean just the opposite. For example, the Age Discrimination in Employment Act of 1967 suggests a bill designed to protect older workers when in fact it allows employers to force employees to waive their right to sue if they want to collect severance payments following a layoff.

[8] My comments in this section benefit from an article written by Elizabeth Williamson and Damian Paletta, "Ban on Pet Provisions Proves too much for Lawmakers," in *The Wall Street Journal*, May 20, 2010.

Both political parties said they would keep this legislation pure and not attach to it other unrelated provisions benefiting one legislator's district, agenda or big financial supporter. Of course, that is not what happened. Over 300 supplemental provisions eventually were inserted into RAFSA though not all of them survived the bills ultimate passage. Among the items attached to the bill were the following:

- A condemnation of the military government of Myanmar.
- A bill to force buyers of minerals purchased in the Democratic Republic of Congo to certify that funds did not go to groups fighting in the region.
- A bill to stop the Environmental Protection Agency from forcing lead paint removers to be certified until every state had a program to train removers.
- A bill to outlaw data processing by prison inmates when the data contains individual's Social Security numbers.

With it being so easy for legislators to ride the coattails of critical legislation and thereby obtain approval for nonessential and possibly harmful bills, it becomes very difficult to weed out and pass only essential legislation and to separate out the pointless, frivolous or the harmful. The title of this section refers of course to the famous expression about hot dogs: "fewer people would eat hot dogs if they knew what went into them." The same is true about government. Legislation gets passed by attachment as in the example above, by horse trading of votes whereby two legislators each votes for the others pet bill and by arm twisting by party leaders. Other legislation is passed by "unanimous consent" wherein individual votes are not recorded and instead bills are simply stamped "passed." Perhaps most disconcerting are the empty Congressional chambers while Congress is in session debating legislation.

So many bills are filed that it is impossible for anyone to read all of them let alone intelligently debate them. While legislators have congressional assistants and substantial

15

budgets, it is probably true too that few legislators actually know what they are voting on all the time. Maybe like hot dogs, which many scientists tell us are not actually healthy food items, our system of legislation is making our nation sick.

How Highways Ran Over Cities

A number of examples fight for the distinction of being the most damaging or horrifying governmental unintended consequence. One contender is the legislation that led to the demise of many American cities. There are approximately 19,400 municipal governments in the US and 58 cities with populations in excess of 300,000. Most have struggled with a variety of social and economic ills. Recalling back to just 1950 reveals a very different picture. Cities were vibrant and bustling.

In 1956 everything changed. Congress passed the Federal-Aid Highway Act which is also known as the National Interstate and Defense Highway System Act of 1956. For President Dwight D. Eisenhower this legislation was a highlight of his administration. Eisenhower's hope, acquired during his years in Europe where he saw the autobahn in Germany, was to build a highway system to facilitate troop movements and the delivery of emergency supplies. Industry perceived a highway system as a means to promote the efficient delivery of goods across the country and recognized how the roads would compete with the nation's expensive railroads. American car manufacturers lobbied heavily for this legislation too. Since 1956 nearly 50,000 miles of highways and millions of automobiles and trucks have been built in the US. [9]

---

[9] In 2011 dollars, it is estimated that the Interstate Highway System cost approximately $213 billion over a 40 year span. To put this number into perspective, the Apollo moon landing is estimated to

The nation's highway system accomplished the military security goals envisioned by President Eisenhower. But what damage came in its wake? People suddenly had the ability to live in the suburbs and to drive into the urban core. Families abandoned the cities and moved to newly constructed suburban communities with backyards and front porches. Eventually, as the first round of suburbs filled up, outer suburban rings were added that included commercial and industrial zones alleviating the need for suburbanites to ever drive into the city. With the diminution of their tax base as higher income residents and jobs fled, cities entered a deadly cycle of decay. Did anyone in Congress consider the unintended consequence of its decision to approve and fund Eisenhower's dream?[10]

The city of Worcester Massachusetts suffered a different sort of injury at the hands of the highway system. Anticipating the construction of the Massachusetts Turnpike, which was to run from Boston all the way to the New York State line as part of the interstate highway system, and fearing its impact on the city, Worcester's city fathers successfully lobbied to have the turnpike skirt the town (there are no direct exits to this day leading into the city) in an effort to preserve the city's business center. Their successful lobbying effort led to an unintended consequence within an unintended consequence. The world passed Worcester by. Worcester soon stopped being the second largest city in New England. Without an access point for highway travelers to enter the city or for goods to move from the city onto the highway the town center decayed.

---

have cost $164 billion. See, "Budget Behemoths: Big-Ticket Government Projects, in 2011 Dollars," *The Wall Street Journal*, May 26, 2011. This article also puts into perspective the extraordinary size of the $787 billion fiscal stimulus package signed by President Obama on February 17, 2009.

[10] An excellent academic paper on this topic is "Did Highways Cause Suburbanization," Nathaniel Baum-Snow, *The Quarterly Journal of Economics*, Vol. 122, No. 2, May 2007.

Worcester's politicians correctly anticipated the monumental impact that the highway system would have on the town but were unable to find a benign solution.

Thinking then of the two questions posed earlier, was it possible for a defense transportation system to be established without simultaneously destroying American cities and was the net effect of the policy beneficial, the conclusions are clearly mixed. The 1950s and the Cold War aroused the passions and fears of most Americans. Normal families constructed bomb shelters in their backyards, stockpiled provisions in case of a nuclear war, and for the most part approved of the military-industrial complex. Was inaction on the highway project a possibility? Probably not. The highway system improved the logistical functionality of our defense apparatus. On the other hand, alternative designs may have achieved similar goals while being more sensitive to its impact on American cities

To answer the second question whether the highway system has led to a better, safer, cleaner or otherwise improved America, the answer depends upon one's perspective. A large fraction of the population would probably argue that they could not live without the convenience and relative inexpensive transportation alternatives afforded to them by the system. Urban commuters, retired travelers, parents shuttling kids to after-school activities, and medical personnel to name just a few groups would probably defend the highway system as we know it. In contrast, urban dwellers, mass transit advocates, architectural aficionados, and sustainability advocates would probably argue that the highway system was counterproductive and destructive. Without a highway system our dependence on foreign crude oil would be substantially lessened. Had perfect foresight been used to perform the decision-making calculus at the time the legislation was debated, it is uncertain whether the legislation in its current form would have been enacted.

The death of the American City is not entirely the responsibility of Eisenhower and his highway system. Other federal legislation played a key role too. The Federal Housing Authority (established in 1934) for some reason redlined inner city neighborhoods as being unsuitable for mortgages causing their property values to plunge. Redlining was made illegal by the Fair Housing Act of 1968. In addition, the passage in 1944 of the GI Bill guaranteed Veterans Administration mortgages to returning servicemen and further stimulated the move to suburbanization. Finally, Title One of the Housing Act of 1949 gave city's Federal dollars (2/3rds of the total amount required) to acquire areas referred to as slums and to raze buildings in a policy called "urban renewal." Many of these properties were inhabitable and in today's culture architecturally unique. The demolished buildings were replaced by unsightly public housing projects that served as breeding grounds for gangs, mayhem, and the dissolution of the inner city family structure.[11]

Michael Milken[12] points out that the government's enablement of low cost mortgages with fixed low interest rates and 30 year terms encouraged the production of larger homes in distant suburbs; he notes that within a generation the average home size increased from 1,200 square feet to approximately 2,500 square feet despite the fact that family size were shrinking. Bigger houses use more energy to heat, cool, and light and require more land stimulating the move to distant suburbs and more highways. Without adequate mass transit in the suburbs people purchased bigger cars which use more energy thereby contributing to a secondary unintended consequence, the energy crisis.

---

[11] An excellent discussion of this and other urban tales can be found in the book *Bricks and Mortals*, Samuel Zipp, Oxford University Press, 2010.

[12] See Michael Milken "Toward a New American Century," *The Wall Street Journal*, October 7, 2010.

How Government Encouraged the 2007 Housing Bust

Finger-pointing rarely does any good, and most stories have two sides. But in the case of the recent great recession, 2007-2009, the culprit may be easier to identify than usual. Start by noting that from time immemorial economies have gone through cycles of boom and bust. Some of the busts have been worse than others but few in modern times can compare to the depth and duration experienced recently. A partial explanation for the magnitude of the recent recession is the near total collapse of a sector of the housing market that would not have existed without government programs. Metaphorically, the government threw gasoline onto a burning fire: the gasoline came in the form of billions of dollars in mortgages underwritten for poor borrowers and the burning fire was a growing economy poised for its next natural slowdown.

In 1977 Congress passed the Community Reinvestment Act (CRA). Following decades of redlining in bank lending, CRA was designed to reverse years of lending discrimination to low income communities. Supervisory agencies were mandated to encourage financial institutions that offered FDIC insurance to lend to their local community in a manner consistent with safe and sound operations. The prior section of this book, "How the Highways Ran Over our Cities", recounted how government activities encouraged the demise of American cities. CRA was designed to reverse that process and to help cities rebuild. What government destroyed it would now try to fix.

Legislation after 1977 related to the CRA strengthened the powers of community groups to influence bank lending practices. A study by the US Department of the Treasury in 2000 reported that in 305 US cities between the years 1993 - 1998, $467 billion in mortgages were written to low and median income borrowers by lenders regulated by

CRA.[13] Janet Yellen, then president of the Federal Reserve Bank of San Francisco, defended the practice arguing that independent mortgage companies, not regulated by CRA, wrote twice as many mortgages to low income and median income borrowers as did CRA regulated banks and thrifts. In any event, the floodgates had been opened and money poured into the subprime mortgage sector.[14]

Congress wasn't done. In 1992, Congress encouraging Fannie Mae and Freddie Mac to increase their purchases of mortgages designed for low and moderate income borrowers.[15] This request was not unusual and was in keeping with a policy that believed that home ownership was an important route out of the ghetto. Not thinking that encouragement was enough, in 1996 the Department of Housing and Urban Development (otherwise known as HUD) gave Fannie Mae and Freddie Mac an explicit target that required 42% of their mortgages to have been initiated by individuals whose income fell below the median for their local area; the target went to 50% in 2000 and 52% in 2005! HUD even created a category of mortgages called special affordable loans for borrowers with incomes less than 60% of the median income in their local area. Lenders were targeted to make 12% of their mortgages in the special affordable category starting in 1996, rising to 20% in 2000 and then 22% in 2005. Had the housing bubble not burst the requirement would have gone to 28% in 2008.[16] Being

---

[13] Litan, Robert E. Nicolas P. Retsinas, Eric S. Belsky, Susan White Haag, "The Community Reinvestment Act After Financial Modernization: A Baseline Report," US Department of the Treasury, April 19, 2000, pp 16–17. http://www.treas.gov/press/releases/docs/crareport.pdf.
[14] See Harlan Platt, "Where Did All the Liquidity Go" *Real Estate Finance,* June, 2010, where the securitization market for subprime loans is discussed and the consequences of the ending of that market on the ability of banks to lend further is discussed.
[15] Russell Roberts, "How Government Stoked the Mania," *The Wall Street Journal*, October 3, 2008.
[16] Ibid.

diligent and obedient servants of the government, Fannie Mae and Freddie Mac met all of these targets. Billions of dollars of subprime and adjustable rate loans were made to borrowers whose creditworthiness would never have passed muster without the government's interdiction into the workings of the financial markets.

By this point the fire in the real estate market was stoked. But it's hard to keep a good Congress from passing more legislation ignorant of any unintended consequence that might arise in its wake. The Taxpayer Relief Act of 1997 quadrupled the tax free portion of housing capital gains: the amount rose from $125,000 to $500,000. Meanwhile the Federal Reserve maintained an unprecedented low interest rate environment as a result of its fears of economic stagnation. Mortgage interest rates followed the federal-funds rate down thereby reducing the cost of home ownership. By this point the fire had gone from hot to scalding and the real estate market was bubbling and frothing. It was time for the unintended consequences.

Trouble started when subprime and Alt-A borrowers began to default on their mortgages in mass. The long accepted theory that real estate prices never decline was challenged by the sheer volume of loan defaults. That theory was probably "almost" true as long as the real estate market remained orderly and without government interference. But a massive wave of defaults heavily concentrated in certain regions, led real estate prices to crumble causing a cascade of further defaults. The unintended consequence of 50 years of government encouragement of home ownership as a social policy was that upwards of 20% of homeowners had insufficient incomes to live in their homes and once they could no longer be bailed out by selling their home at a higher price than they had paid, the merry-go-round came to stop.

How Pandering to Constituents Creates a Politically Unstable Situation

Prior to President Franklin Delano Roosevelt and the New Deal it was extremely unpleasant to be poor or indigent. The social safety net was just 6 inches off of the ground and many families suffered from homelessness, hunger, and poor health. Since the inaugural programs of the New Deal began in 1933 the number and variety of governmental transfer programs aiding the poor have proliferated and grown. (See the section below entitled "How Unlike Old Soldiers Government Largess Never Fades Away", for a discussion on the inability to control or terminate governmental programs). In addition to cash transfers (such as needs-based assistance programs and family allowances) expenditures include food-based programs, energy subsidies, employment opportunities in public work programs, and fee waivers. Arguably the list should also include partially supported programs such as Social Security, Medicare and Medicaid since this section refers to the way politicians manipulate voters by inducing their support through generous governmental benefits.

It will always be the case that it is better to be rich than poor (at least I hope so). But since the mid-1930s the plight of the less fortunate has vastly improved. The problem is that paying for these kindnesses doesn't come cheaply. This section is not concerned with the cost of these programs on a specific basis, that topic is approached elsewhere in this book, but rather on how they have created a duality amongst citizens: those who get and those who give. In 2010, "nearly half of all Americans live in a household in which someone receives government benefits, more than at any time in history." [17] Moreover, 45% of American households pay no income tax. What you have then is a nearly perfect bifurcation of the population into two equally sized groups with one being taxed to give benefits to the other. No unwritten law demarcates the correct split into the givers and getters. Instead, it evolves in each society based on factors such as the growth in earnings, the demographics of old and young, the rate of immigration of less well educated populations, and the ability of politicians to curry voter favor with expensive benefits without someone asking how they plan to pay for them. [18]

The unintended consequence created by this behavior is an unsound political balance with nearly half of the voters preferring one party because they are more generous with benefits and with nearly half of the population preferring the other party because they advocate lower taxes. Nearly half is not quite 50%. Having two nearly halves means that there is perhaps 10% of the population that controls the outcome of an election. Consider the last two elections. In 2008 President Obama promised change by which he meant more benefits for union workers, retirees, and other supporters of the Democratic Party. His appeal resonated sufficiently with the critical 10% of the population that his party carried the day. Then in 2010 the Republicans campaigned on ending the Obama health initiative, controlling taxes, and making progress against the deficit. The swing 10% of the population liked what they heard and put the Republicans in control of the House of Representatives.

---

[17] Sarah Murray, "Obstacle to Deficit Cutting: a Nation on Entitlements," The Wall Street Journal, September 15, 2010.

[18] It should be said in all fairness that the percentage of income the average American receives from the government is far lower than the similar proportion in most of the industrial West. In fact, the average American receives only one third the amount of money from the government as does the average person in France or Sweden. See Sarah Murray's article, Ibid, for more data on this topic.

The traditional view was that outcomes such as these last two elections were good for the country as no single party permanently dominates the electoral process. Maybe that view was correct in the past, but it no longer holds. Exactly who each party must pander to becomes clearer as the number of swing voters declines. In the extreme, if there was just one swing voter and the other voters split equally 49.99999% to each party then the sole swing voter is the only one who matters. As each party raises their ante giving more and more to the swing voter, election outcomes rock back and forth between the two philosophies.

Some may argue that this development is not bad for the country, and they may be right, but it is certainly an unintended consequence of the movement in American politics to establish a culture breed on the receipt of entitlements bereft of the matter of how to pay for them.

How Governmental Lifestyle Restrictions Bring Misery

Governmental prohibitions intended to change personal behavior have ruined more lives and wasted more money than any other legislation. The damage results from unintended consequences that follow the enactment of life-style legislation. Substances forbidden in the US have included alcohol and a variety of drugs, while behavioral dictums have included gambling and prostitution among others. In the case of alcohol, prohibition began in 1920 and ended in 1933. This legislation followed similar prohibitions in other countries starting in parts of Canada in 1907. The US was late compared to other countries to restrict the consumption of drugs. The first prohibition against drug use in the US was an ordinance passed in San Francisco in 1875 outlawing opium dens. In 1914 the Harrison Act was passed requiring sellers of opiates and cocaine to be federally licensed. The Marijuana Tax Act passed Congress without opposition in 1937.

America's unquenchable thirst for drugs and restriction against them has had an unintended consequence of creating an unprecedented business opportunity for smugglers and other entrepreneurs notably in Mexico and South America. Along with millionaires and billionaires, the prohibition has caused a human bloodbath in Mexico and elsewhere. There were more than 5,000 drug related murders in Mexico in 2008, another 6,500 in 2009, and 34,600 in the four years since President Felipe Calderon took office.[19] [20] Efforts by President Calderon to use the army to combat smugglers and their murderous ways have proved largely futile. In one stark indication of how deadly the situation is, Mexican police went to investigate an apparent abduction and instead found a pit containing the bodies of 59 victims of the drug gangs.[21] If anything governmental efforts have simply made the smugglers more ingenious and creative. The situation is not much different than when sand bags are used in an effort to control a flooding river; the water surges around the bags and finds a new route.

Another unintended consequence of the effort to keep drugs out of the US has been that smugglers have developed alternative markets for their products near the US border for times when their product cannot cross the border safely. The city of Ciudad Juarez in Mexico is one example. In a few years the city has gone from being a transit point for drugs into the US to becoming a major consumption point. Violence accompanied the transition. In 2009 this city of 1.3

---

[19] See Jo Tuckman and Ed Vulliamy, "Mexico's Drug Wars Rage Out of Control," *The Guardian*, March 24, 2010.
[20] Randall C Archbold, "In Mexico Drug War, Massacres but Official Claims of Progress," *The New York Times*, February 1, 2011.
[21] Katherine Corcoran, "Mexican Cops Checking Abductions Find Mass Graves," Associated Press, April 7, 2011.

million people endured 12 murders a day as rival gangs fought for retail customers.

Profits earned by the 20 largest <u>ethical</u> drug manufacturers amounted to $110 billion in 2006 with these firms employing 1,342,700 workers.[22] Profit estimates for the illegal drug market are harder to come by. One estimate for 1998 when the problem was less severe, by Abt Associates, concluded that expenditures on illegal drugs by Americans equaled $65 billion.[23] Expenditures are not the same thing as profits. More recently, the PBS Networks' Frontline program has estimated a worldwide $400 billion global business in illegal drug. One authority has estimated that drug traffickers have profit margins of 300%.[24] Coupling these two estimates together suggests a worldwide profit of nearly $300 billion for drug traffickers which far surpass the worldwide profitability of the 20 largest pharmaceutical companies. With profits like these, smugglers buy off politicians, police officers, and journalist. And all of this arises because some politicians a long time ago thought they could pass a law which would change human behavior. Too bad they didn't consider the inevitability of unintended consequences.

A scholarly article by Jeffrey Miron and Katherine Waldock details the enormous financial cost of the government's misconstrued efforts to prohibit marijuana consumption. [25] They estimate that drug legalization would reduce government expenditures by over $41 billion annually with 62% of the savings accruing to state and local

---

[22] Data obtained from "Pharmaceutical Industry," *Wikipedia*, September 30, 2010.

[23] Source: Abt Associates Inc., "What America's Users Spend on Illegal Drugs," 1988-98.

[24] Richard Davenport-Hines, *The Pursuit of Oblivion*, W.W. Norton & Company, 2001.

[25] Jeffrey Miron and Katherine Waldock, *The Budgetary Impact of Ending Drug Prohibition*, Cato Institute, September 27, 2010.

governments. Of this amount approximately $8.7 billion is associated with the legalization of marijuana. In addition, they estimate tax revenues from drug legalization at approximately $46.7 billion per year with 18.6% of this being taxes on marijuana. Among the strongest voices opposing drug legalization are those who make their living prosecuting, defending, and otherwise restricting the freedom of others. An unintended consequence of most legislation is that once enacted it remains on the books forever.

The prohibition against marijuana has had a disaster unintended consequence upon the black community. A report issued by the Marijuana Arrest Research Project [26] in 2010 suggests that arrests for marijuana possession and sale in the black community exceed those in the white community by sevenfold. People arrested for these offenses have a hard time getting jobs, borrowing money, or obtaining Federal aid. Advocates of a no drug policy would probably on the one hand argue that these individuals deserve their punishment because they broke the law while simultaneously bemoaning the economic deprivation in the black community. Some of this deprivation results from the secondary consequences of enforcement of drug prohibition legislation.

The Marijuana Arrest Research Project report also says that in the past 10 years over 500,000 people have been arrested, in just the state of California, for marijuana possession. More than 80% of these arrests were nonwhite individuals. Charles Blow notes in an article in *The New York Times* following the release of the report that according to the National Survey on Drug Use and Health that white Americans have a higher marijuana usage rate than do either

---

[26] The Marijuana Arrest Research Project, Harry G. Levine, Jon B. Gettman, Loren Siegel, *Targeting Blacks for Marijuana Possession: Arrests of African Americans in California, 2004-08*, June 29, 2010.

blacks or Hispanics. [27] The zealous pursuit of minor drug infractions among minority individuals is responsible for at least a portion of the poverty and hopelessness in that community.

Efforts to eradicate or control illicit drugs often have surprising unintended consequences. One of the most pernicious of all drugs is methamphetamines (meth). Meth is a highly addictive pharmaceutical known to give its users feelings of euphoria, higher self-esteem, and increased libidos. [28] Users also face a form of schizophrenia, cardiovascular damage and a higher risk of developing Parkinson's disease. [29] Photos of the human devastation wrought on meth users by this powerful drug are heart wrenching (see http://www.oregonlive.com/news/oregonian/photos /gallery.ssf?cgi-bin/view_gallery.cgi/olive/view_gallery.ata?g_id=2927). Few but the staunchest of libertarians might suggest that the government not control the use and distribution of meth. With that said, recent successes in Mexico cracking down on meth labs have had an unintended consequence of its own. That consequence is the return of meth labs to the US, notably in California and Georgia. [30]

An unintended consequence caused by the prohibition of alcohol was that it delivered a two-fisted blow

---

[27] Charles M. Blow, "Smoke and Horrors," *The New York Times*, October 23, 2010.

[28] Avram H Mack, Richard J Frances, and Sheldon I. Miller, 2005, *Clinical Textbook of Addictive Disorders, Third Edition*, New York: The Guilford Press.

[29] S Darke, S Kaye, R McKetin, and J Duflou, 2008, "Major Physical and Psychological Harms of Methamphetamine Use," *Drug Alcohol Review* 27 (3): 253–62, May.

[30] Justin Scheck, "Meth Labs Make Return to US," *The Wall Street Journal*, December 4-5, 2010.

to American cuisine.[31] Wine and other alcoholic beverages are often key ingredients in the production of tasty meals. William Grimes argues that NYC turned into a hick-food town following prohibition and stayed that way until 1960. Beyond the loss of a key ingredient, prohibition removed the single most profitable item from the menus of American restaurants. Without alcoholic beverages to serve and with alcohols removal from the chef's palette American restaurants became mundane and ordinary. Other alcohol related unintended consequences are well documented in movies like the *Untouchables* which depicted how criminal gangs supplied alcohol, made fortunes, and killed off their competitors. Government restrictions or no government restriction, people kept on drinking.

How Efforts to Control Population Backfire

The idea that nothing is more sacrosanct than one's bedroom has escaped the population control lobby.[32] How many children a family should have would seem to be the providence of only two people. Yet governments spend enormous time and resources interjecting their views into this bedroom decision process. While government strictures in certain countries have in fact controlled population growth their impact on total global population has been overshadowed by the extraordinary negative correlation between wealth and family size. As wealth rises, family size falls. This is almost universally true.[33] Governments that

---

[31] See William Grimes, *Appetite City: The Culinary History of New York*, North Point Press, 2010.

[32] A wonderful review of the history of population control is found in the book by Matthew Connelly, *Fatal Misconception*, Belknap, 2010.

[33] A contrary example is when Ireland's economy accelerated its growth rate in the late 1990s and early 2000s, there was a mini baby boom.

want to reduce population growth should find ways to improve the standard of living in their own countries and leave bedroom decisions in the bedroom.

In 1978 the Chinese government introduced a policy of one-child per family. The stated reason was the need to control a burgeoning population and thereby limit environmental problems and improve social welfare. The Chinese government estimates that 400 million births have been averted by the policy. China's rapid economic development and associated growth in income has contributed some portion of the reduction in births though government sanctions, heavy fines, social stigmas, and possibly forced abortions and sterilizations were the principle agents. Adherents to the theories of Thomas Malthus, the author in 1798 of *An Essay on the Principle of Population*, might defend the Chinese form of population control. Not being versed in unintended consequences though they would not reckon with the enormous social damage caused by governmental interference in bedroom politics.

The Chinese Academy of Social Science estimates that in the year 2020 nearly 24 million Chinese men will be unable to find a spouse. [34] Now wait a minute you might say. If a country reduces births from 5 children per couple to one then logically births should still be divided approximately 50% boys and 50% of girls. But that is not what happens. Countries with an uncertain social safety net have long relied upon the eldest male child to care for his parents in their old age. If a family can only have one child then logically they want to have a boy child in order to avoid destitution as they age. The ratio of births in China has dramatically shifted to 46% girls and 54% boys. [35] The unintended consequence of a one-child policy is the disruption of the normal birth

---

[34] "China Faces Growing Gender Imbalance," *BBC News*, January 11, 2010.
[35] Ibid.

gender split. What's a few percent you might ask? Well in a country the size of China that amounts to 24 million unmarried men.

When a country has excess males in its population something has to give. A report from the Chinese Academy of Social Science notes that forced prostitution appears to be rampant in parts of China.[36] Another outcome that may surface in China would be polyandry or the marriage of one woman to several men. Polyandry is more likely to arise in rural areas where intense physical labor makes single unit families more difficult to sustain.

The extraordinary decline in the Chinese birth rate -- from five births per woman in 1970, to three births in 1979, to 1.7 births in 2007 -- has produced major unintended consequences.[37] The Chinese population has fallen below the "net reproduction rate" of 1.0, which is defined as the average number of daughters born to each female, required for a steady population size. Consequently, the total Chinese population will begin to fall in the not too distant future[38] and more importantly the working age population will soon begin to decline.[39] Not only will this affect China's ability to be the low cost producer in the world but it will also recreate the population problem that is currently befuddling Japan wherein too few employed individuals are supporting an overabundance of retired nonworking people. This dramatic change in population mix is one of the reasons that Japan has been recession-bound for nearly two decades. The unintended consequence of dramatically and permanently altering the population dynamic will play itself out in the future in China. It is likely to produce a stagnant economy burdened with massive social obligations.

---

[36] Ibid.

[37] Nicholas Eberstadt, "China's One-Child Mistake, "*The Wall Street Journal*, September 17, 2007.

[38] As soon as 2030, according to Eberstadt.

[39] Ibid.

There is a natural change in the population growth rate as countries grow wealthier. Wealth is rapidly rising in China, notably in larger cities such as Beijing. [40] Had the communist government of China not imposed the one-child birth rule but instead had it adopted quasi capitalism earlier than it is likely that a similar population reduction would have resulted not from coercion but from choice. More importantly, the change would have been more gradual and the negative consequences anticipated for China in the next generation would have been less severe.

Infant girls are also missing in India. The National Population Stabilization Fund in India reports that selective abortion of female fetuses is widespread and worrisome. [41] In 2011 only 914 girls were born in India for every 1000 male births. Unlike China, whose infanticide is driven by a restriction on multiple births, the Indian experience appears to be confined to wealthier families who have decided to have fewer children in total and want the firstborn to be a male. Like China, the unintended consequence of this abnormal family planning method is the likelihood that these male offspring will have no one to wed when they reach maturity.

Throughout the Western world reduced population growth, generally due to improving living standards and work opportunities, will radically affect economies long into the future. These are unintended consequences. As Nicholas Eberstadt and Hans Groth argue declining birth rates will result in, "stagnant populations, shrinking workforces, steadily increasing pension-age populations, and ballooning social spending commitments." [42] The ramifications of these

---

[40] Ibid.

[41] Jim Yardley, "As Wealth and Literacy Rise in India, Report Says, So Do Sex-Selective Abortions," *The New York Times*, May 25, 2011.

[42] Nicolas Eberstadt and Hans Groth, "Time for 'Demographic Stress Tests'" *The Wall Street Journal*, November 27, 2010.

demographic changes will make it difficult for countries to maintain their GDP levels and to remain fiscally solvent.

How Price Controls Hurt Intended Beneficiaries

Whenever a shortage of goods arises well-meaning governments seek to alleviate the problem by implementing price controls on producers or suppliers. Governments ignore the fact that price controls bring forth unintended consequences. The unintended consequences start when the price controls lower prices below their market clearing level. Lower prices translate into lower profits. Profits provide a signal to producers; higher profits lead them to supply more goods while lower profits reduce supply. Strict price controls forcing price rollbacks may completely shut down a marketplace. Less severe price restrictions may induce suppliers to reduce quality or to not add to their supply capability. Price restrictions rarely help their intended beneficiaries. Examples of failed price controls include gasoline from October 1973 through March 1974, apartment rentals in New York City and Berkeley California, and electricity prices in California.

Gasoline

On November 27, 1973 President Richard Nixon signed the Emergency Petroleum Allocation Act. This law authorized governmental controls over petroleum price, production, allocation, and marketing. The impetus for this legislation was the dramatic rise in petroleum prices that followed the Arab - Israeli war of 1973. From the period building up to the war and then shortly thereafter oil prices rose from approximately $3.00 per barrel in 1973 to about $12.00 in 1974 and nearly $40.00 a barrel in 1982. Such a dramatic price increase created hardship and dislocation on major energy consumers: residential customers in the

Northeast, large industrial consumers in the Midwest, and automobile motorists. The pain was palpable as for example when gasoline prices rose from a low of 10¢ a gallon up to 60¢ or beyond per gallon. The feeling was that government needed to do something but since it could not replace the oil that was withheld from the market by OPEC producers it did something else namely imposed price controls.

Several months earlier in August 1973 President Nixon's Cost of Living Council created a two tier structure for oil prices. The first tier was oil that was already discovered and its price was constrained to the price in March of 1973 plus 35¢. The second tier was newly discovered oil and its was allowed to be sold at the market price The idea behind the two tiers was to promote new oil discoveries but instead what it did as an unintended consequence was to discourage the sale of old oil thereby creating a scarcity. Producers were unwilling to sell old oil for as little as a dollar a barrel when new production perhaps just a short distance away could be sold for five are 10 times more. Alternative energy supplies such as natural gas were not available as a substitute for the missing petroleum since the price of natural gas had been controlled by government edict since the 1950s and as a consequence natural gas supplies had been falling. Today after natural gas deregulation the fuel is so abundant that new and creative uses for it are being found such as automobiles powered by natural gas.

The oil supply shortage and the government's misdirected response to it led to rationing as the way to allocate the limited supply of oil to those who wanted to buy it at the artificially low price. The government imposed odd - even rationing days wherein drivers were only allowed to fill up their vehicles with gasoline on days corresponding to the last digit in their license plate. That system didn't work and cars were lining up for blocks at gas stations to buy fuel. The

American Automobile Association estimated that at one point 20% of American cars had no fuel at all. [43]

Today with natural gas prices unregulated there is a dramatic surplus of gas supplies in the US. Producers have explored and discovered gas in huge quantities where it had not been anticipated. Their efforts were motivated by profits. Some made fortunes with their discoveries others whose discovery efforts were futile went broke. But America got natural gas. Had price controls not been imposed during this earlier energy crisis, energy usage would have declined substantially as higher prices forced consumers to conserve. Governmental assistance in the form of cash grants could have been used to assist low income Americans. In addition, producers would have quickly generated new supplies to fuel American cars, industry and homes. Instead price controls were implemented and a series of unintended consequences caused pain and hardship throughout the economy.

Rent Control

In 1943 the City of New York enacted a system of rent control laws that are still on the books. Today over one million apartments in NYC are rent stabilized. [44] The system is complex and has many caveats but basically certain buildings and certain apartments are controlled so that their rents are not allowed to rise to market levels. The unintended consequence of such a program is that rent controlled units are often occupied by relatively wealthy inhabitants (all things considered landlords prefer wealthier tenants) while others with lower income are forced to compete for the reduced supply of free market apartments thereby raising their prices. As with any system with governmental control over a marketplace there is a great

---

[43] David Frum, 2000, *How We Got Here: The '70s*. New York, New York: Basic Books.
[44] Jeremy W Peters, "Assembly Passes Rent-Regulation Revisions Opposed by Landlords," *The New York Times*. February 3, 2009

deal of abuse. For example, Charles Rangel a powerful member of the US Congress was the tenant of four rent stabilized apartments. [45] Similarly, Bianca Jagger, the ex-wife of Rolling Stone Mick Jagger, was forced to pay over $708,000 in back rent and fines to her landlord after occupying a rent controlled two-bedroom apartment for nearly 20 years. [46] It took that long for the courts to rule that NYC was not Ms. Jagger's permanent residence as required under rent control laws.

California Electricity Prices

The California Public Utilities Commission in 2000 changed the rules defining how it regulated the prices charged by electricity utilities. Perversely the commission deregulated wholesale electricity prices but maintained strict retail price regulations. That is, the cost of supplying electricity was unlimited but these costs could not be passed on to consumers. The artificially low retail price of electricity encouraged continued consumption by consumers and discouraged their practicing conservation measures. Meanwhile, deregulated energy producers manipulated the market to drive up the cost of electricity to the utilities. Blackouts ensued and eventually Pacific Gas &Electric, one of the largest energy producers in California, filed for bankruptcy protection. The unintended consequences of this misguided legislation is that energy supplies became scare in California.

Summary

Markets work. Artificial price controls distort markets leading to shortages. Price controls give producers or suppliers information that their product has a lower value than the actual value ascribed to it by consumers. For example, a consumer might be willing to pay $10 for

---

[45] "Evicting Bianca Jagger," *The New York Times*, July 30, 2010.
[46] Ibid.

something but if price controls restrict that product's price to $7 then producers will not supply enough products to the market and the consumer who is willing to pay $10 for it doesn't get any. Consumer's lucky enough to get product at the limit price of $7 support price controls because it has saved them money (people in rent controlled apartments love the policy); while consumers who are unable to get product (because the supply has been sold out) are unhappy. With rent control, elected officials don't face the wrath of unhappy consumers because those unable to rent an apartment move elsewhere.

How Price Controls Promote Other Problems

Governmental decisions have a nasty way of reappearing years later to inflict harm. When enacted they may seem to accomplish their intended goal but in the long term unintended consequences arise. An example of this delayed effect is the system of wage and price controls imposed by the federal government during World War II because at the time everything was in short supply. Those controls were designed to avoid profiteering during the war. Imposing wage and price controls on an entire nation is a major undertaking. It requires the creation of a bureaucracy and the dissemination of bureaucratic decisions. One such edict during the war was the decision to exempt from wage and price controls health insurance provided by employers to employees.[47]

With wages under tight government control and with companies desperate to attract workers into factories for the war effort, companies creatively began to offer generous health insurance plans to their workers. In some cases, company provided health insurance included coverage for

---

[47] Gerald F. Seib, "US Psyche Bedevils Health Effort," *The Wall Street Journal*, Page A2, August 4, 2009.

worker's families as well. When the war ended health benefits remained behind.

The unintended consequence of wage and price controls during the Second World War was the acceptance by most workers in the US of the notion that company offered health insurance was a right. Prior to the war, workers purchased and paid for their own insurance if they wanted it though in reality few actually did. Today it's just the opposite. Most discussion of health insurance concerns the 50 million US residents who in 2010 lacked insurance for at least a portion of the year. Perversely, there is no questioning about the 84.6% of the population with insurance or of who pays for it. Although employers are not alone in providing this insurance they account for a major share of it. If health insurance premiums were not tax deductible fewer companies would offer them.

Compounding this unintended consequence was the fact that the health insurance provided through collective bargaining agreements, notably in the auto and steel industries, generally required no co-payment by the insured. That is, a person could get medical attention in the doctor's office or in a hospital and pay almost nothing out of their own pocket. With somebody else paying the bill, people have grown accustomed to treating medical care as a free good. There's nothing wrong with free medical care when you are the person who is ill but when an entire society treats medicine as a free good for which they are entitled to any and all services, the entire economy can become insolvent. If employer-provided health insurance had more realistic deductibles, consumers would be more careful with their health spending.

An almost unlimited demand for medical care with a near fixed supply results in higher prices being charged by doctors and hospital. Medical professionals before World War II earned higher salaries than the average worker, but nowhere near the wage premium earned by doctors today.

Insurance companies and the government do not pay full price for medical services but rather they pay a negotiated price; the ignominy of paying full price is reserved for those without insurance. More is said on healthcare in Chapter 7. In this section we have seen how one government decision, wage and price controls, had an unintended consequence of turning health insurance into a right expected by all workers and then of pushing medical prices upwards.

How Protecting One Worker Hurts Another

Pendulums swing back and forth. As described in the Biblical saying, "the weak shall inherit the earth" sometimes those at the bottom become those at the top. A change of near Biblical proportions has occurred in the past 100 years in the relative position of public sector vs. private sector workers. Previously it was private sector employees who commanded the best wages and benefits. Their brethren in the public sector not only had lower wages but they lacked adequate job security and pensions. That has all changed dramatically.

A century ago public sector employees were nearly second class citizens. This changed dramatically in 1912 with the passage of the Lloyd - LaFollette Act which allowed Federal workers to organize. [48] Then in 1962, public sector employees were given the right to collectively bargain. The unintended consequence of pro-union legislation has been to make public sector employment an aspiration job. Rather than bring income parity to public sector employees, public sector jobs have become gold plated. Most noteworthy have been the pension benefits provided to public sector employees. For example, the former head librarian of the city of San Diego receives over $227,000 a year as an annual

---

[48] Amity Shlaes, "How Government Unions Became so Powerful," *The Wall Street Journal*, September 4, 2010.

retirement allowance. [49] Making matters worse, dismissal of unproductive public employees can be a frustrating process that takes years to complete. [50]

When negotiating contracts with public sector unions, politicians often prefer to provide rich pension benefits rather than expensive salary hikes. The reason for this choice is that future pension obligations will be paid out when the current politician is no longer in office. It becomes somebody else's problem. The problem of deferred responsibility has come home to roost. The pension obligations of cities and states may bankrupt some of them. As of the end of 2009 the average public pension plan was 35% underfunded. [51] The only way this gap can be closed is by increasing taxes on private sector employees or by reducing promised pensions. Reductions in promised pensions are difficult to achieve. For example, Pennsylvania's constitution explicitly prohibits laws that revoke pension benefits. [52]

Another alternative is municipal bankruptcy or Chapter 9 of the bankruptcy code. One condition in the Code is that municipalities can only file for bankruptcy protection if so authorized by their state governments. Currently only 19 states permit municipal bankruptcies. [53] And even then states have restrictions on those bankruptcies that affect the ability of the Code to reduce pension obligations. [54] New

[49] Carl DeMaio, "Report Reveals Excessive Pension Payout in City of San Diego," *San Diego Rostra*, October 4, 2010.
[50] Shlaes, Op cit.
[51] Edward Siedle, "Public Pensions Face Ugly Choices," *Forbes*, November 6, 2009
[52] "Issue Summary Municipal Bankruptcy", Allegheny Institute for Public Policy, January 2010.
[53] Ibid.
[54] Shlaes, Op cit.

York State for example has a constitutional guarantee that pensions will be paid. [55]

The Aesop tale of the lion and the mouse may not hold true in real life. After pulling the thorn from the lion's paw the mouse and the lion became best friends and lived happily ever after. In the modern tale, politicians pulled the thorn from the foot of poorly compensated public sector employees and provided them with job security, high wages, and bankruptcy-proof pension plans. Instead of being best friends forever, the unintended consequence of this largess is that public sector employees may soon bankrupt their mouse.

How Myopic Referenda Create Disaster

In 1978 California voters approved Proposition 13 – the People's Initiative to Limit Property Taxation. The key section of the proposition rolled back assessed property values in the State of California to their 1975 values and only allowed revaluation when the property changed hands or was demolished and rebuilt. The impetus for the Proposition came from two sources. First, was a feeling that government spending in the state was out of control. The proportion of the California workforce employed in the public sector doubled from the 1950s to the end of the 1970s.[56] Second it was felt that older homeowners should not be taxed out of their houses by rising real estate taxes.

The old saying two wrongs don't make a right comes to mind. Simply imposing any change when starting from a

---

[55] Allegheny Institute, Op cit.

[56] J. Citrin, J. and D. Sears, *Tax Revolt: Something for Nothing in California*, Harvard University Press,1985

bad situation doesn't mean that you will be better off.[57] The need for change in California was obvious but too little foresight and ignorance of unintended consequences created a warped Proposition. Had the architects of Proposition 13 been aware of the damage it would cause, they likely would have written it differently. California government was too large and is still too large. In fact some people argue that California's government became larger as a result of Proposition 13.[58] They argue that by limiting tax revenues in local communities the Proposition pushed the State to pick up the shortfall and thereby grow larger itself.

Proposition 13 creates a disincentive to sell property. That is an important unintended consequence. As long as an owner stays in a home its real estate tax cannot increase by more than 2% per annum. Selling a house on one side of the street after having lived in it for 30 years and buying an identical property on the other side of the street could easily double one's property tax bill. The California real estate market is more rigid than those in other states.[59] Many larger homes with three or more bedrooms are occupied by one elderly individual. Not only does this lead to energy inefficiency since these larger homes are space conditioned as if they were occupied by a larger family but it pushes up the cost of home ownership facing young families who are forced to rent rather than buy for a longer time period in California than in other states.[60]

---

[57] This situation represents one of the best examples of what in economics is called the theory of the second best. The theory argues that when there is market failure efforts to change the situation may actually produce negative results.

[58] Joe Mathews and Mark Paul, *California Crackup*, University of California Press. 2010.

[59] Les Picker, "The Lock-in Effect of California's Proposition 13". National Bureau of Economic Research. http://www.nber.org/digest/apr05/w11108.html.

[60] Ibid.

Communities in California desperate for revenue have resorted to other means of taxation. This is a second unintended consequence of the Proposition. The sales tax rate was 6% in 1978 and is now at least 8.25% and is as high as 10.75% when local sales taxes are included. Not only are sales taxes highly regressive but they discourage consumption and property improvement and lead to Internet retail sales. With so many expenditures normally paid for by local government being paid by the state, California is broke despite a maximum income tax rate of 9.3%. Even with the high income tax rate, the state had a budget shortfall of $40 billion in 2008, faced insolvency in 2009, and is confronting a $70 billion shortfall in 2010. California is perceived as being unfriendly to business. When 458 business leaders were polled, California was identified as being the worst state for business by 182 of them while by contrast just 13 cited the State of Texas. [61] Not surprisingly then, in 2010 Toyota moved its auto assembly plant out of California and into Texas. Corporate migration and the loss of jobs further aggravate California's fiscal issues.

Following the passage of Proposition 13, public schools in California which had been top ranked have fallen in perceived quality to 48th nationally. [62] This is a third unintended consequence of the Proposition. Other factors have undoubtedly contributed to this decline, but a stagnant tax base has not allowed communities to maintain the level of spending necessary to preserve education quality.

All in all California appears to be on its deathbed. The legislators and the governor are unable to work together, the unemployment rate is near the top for all states, jobs are leaving, and finger pointing is the game politicians are playing. There are many explanations for the end of the

---

[61] BNET Business Owners, "Texas Tops List of Business-Friendly States," *The Chief Executive*, January/February 2005.
[62] J S McCombs and S J Carroll, "Ultimate Test: Who Is Accountable for Education If Everybody Fails?" *Rand Institute*, Spring 2005.

sunshine state. Proposition 13 is one of the culprits. Did Howard Jarvis and Paul Gann, the unofficial parents of Proposition 13, consider how the Proposition would affect the state in the future? Their immediate goals were met: property taxes on the elderly could no longer be accused of pushing people out of their homes and at least initially government spending was reduced. It is not sufficient to merely address the narrow concerns that impel legislation and voter propositions. When crafting legislative policy it is also necessary to consider unintended consequences. If we are told that that is too difficult then perhaps that legislative proposition should be deferred until the task is easier. The do-no-harm rule should apply to both legislators and drafters of voter propositions.

How Big Government Talks Out of Both Sides of its Mouth

Big government has the potential to be more damaging than smaller governments. One way this comes about is when multiple parts of the government enact rules and regulations that conflict among themselves. In most cases, the implementation of a do-no-harm rule can reduce governmental unintended consequences. However, the rule's beneficial effect may be lost if two parts of the same government promote opposing agendas.

A quintessential example of conflicting government programs is the confusion about the consumption and sale of cheese. Humans have produced cheese for 5,000 years. Relatively easy to make, cheese contains proteins and fat from milk that are solidified by the addition of enzymes. Among its advantages are the facts that cheese is more easily transported and longer-lived than milk.

On the plus side cheese provides calcium, protein, phosphorus and fat. But on the negative side, much of this fat is saturated consisting of dangerous triglycerides. The scientific evidence on the health aspects of saturated fats is mixed. Clinical studies which replace triglycerides with polyunsaturated fats report a reduction in heart disease.[63] Yet meta-analysis studies report no statistically significant relationship between heart disease and saturated fats.[64] The evidence is not clear. Nonetheless, health advocates have persuaded many people to reduce their consumption of cheese. But not everyone has listened to these exhortations. The per capita consumption of cheese in America has tripled to nearly 33 pounds since 1970.[65]

Medical professionals define obesity using the body mass index (BMI).[66] The formula for BMI is relatively simple. Take a person's weight and multiply it by 703 and then divide that quotient by that person's height in inches squared. So for example, a 300 pound person who is 6 feet (72 inches) tall has a BMI of 40.7 = 210,900 divided by 5184. A BMI greater than 40 falls into the worst obesity category, class III. If that same person weighed just 200 pounds their BMI would equal 27.1 which would put them in the overweight but not obese category. Dropping another 50 pounds to 150 pounds lowers the person's BMI to just 20.3 which is considered normal. Just 10% of men aged 20 – 74 had BMI values of 30 or greater in 1960 while nearly 30% did in 2000. Among women in the same age category, the percentage with BMI values of 30 or greater rose from

---

[63] Siri-Tarino PW, Sun Q, Hu FB, Krauss RM, 2010, "Meta-analysis of Prospective Cohort Studies Evaluating the Association of Saturated Fat with Cardiovascular Disease," *The American Journal of Clinical Nutrition* 91 (3): 535–46.

[64] Ibid.

[65] Michael Moss, "While Warning about Fat, US Pushes Cheese Sales," *The New York Times*, November 8, 2010

[66] BMI originated in the 19th century. It was repopularized in Keys, Ancel; Fidanza, F; Karvonen, MJ; Kimura, N; Taylor, HL 1972, "Indices of Relative Weight and Obesity," *Journal of Chronic Disease,* 1 25 (6): 329–43.

approximately 15% in 1960 to about 30% in 2000.[67] While not every obese person is unhealthy the proportion of unhealthy people who are obese is very high. Few if any health advocates recommend obesity. Most recognize that a less obese population would be healthier.

Can we put the two ideas presented in this section together? That is, is the rising level of cheese consumption a cause of the rapid increase in obesity in America? The answer to this question is complex. Other factors undoubtedly play a role. For example, per capita consumption of water has fallen and has been replaced by the consumption of carbonated beverages, fruit drinks, and sports aides; the proportion of meals cooked at home has fallen replaced by meals purchased at fast food restaurants. Consumption of sweeten foods has risen as well. All of these factors and cheese consumption (and other fatty milk products) are probably the principle agents behind the growing obesity problem in America.

Government agencies such as the Center for Disease Control and the Office of the Surgeon General have taken up the clarion call to alert the population to the evident danger in the consumption of too much cheese. Meanwhile, within the government, Dairy Management an agency with a $140 million annual budget works to encourage restaurants to increase the amount of cheese used in their products.[68] Most of Dairy Management's budget is raised from mandatory fees on dairy farmers. By contrast, the Agriculture Department's Center for Nutrition Policy and Promotion has a $6.5 million annual budget to use in its efforts to improve American diets. Outnumbered 20:1 it is not surprising that the less cheese faction is losing.

---

[67] "Healthy Weight, Overweight, and Obesity among US Adults," *National Health and Nutrition Examination Survey*, Center for Disease Control, July 2003.
[68] Moss, op. cit.

The objective here is not to get involved in the health debate over cheese. Instead, it is to note the unintended consequence of a very large government. On the one hand, the government tells people to look to the left and on the other hand it tells them to look to the right. Not surprisingly, the food sold at grocery stores, in restaurants, and in vending machines continues to decline in nutritional value and the health of Americans continues to suffer. The reasoning behind this schizophrenic behavior by the government is fairly obvious too. It confronts demands from disparate parties.

Farmers are a strong political force. [69] Farmer's efforts in Congress to promote their own wellbeing have resulted in a massive bureaucracy geared to the encouragement and promotion of industrial farms. But the government has concerns about health matters as well. Diabetes is an illness associated with obesity. A report from the University of Chicago indicates that the number of diabetic Americans is expected to grow by the year 2034 from 24 million in 2009 to more than 44 million.[70] The medical cost of treating their diabetes is likely to grow from $113 billion annually to $336 billion. The tradeoff between farm incomes and the health of Americans is becoming clearer. At some point the farm lobby will lose its influence. One projection for when that time will come is when the Federal government is bankrupted by the high cost of obesity related medical care.

---

[69] H. Platt, M. Platt, and S. Demirkan, "Does Unemployment Steer Personal and Corporate Bankruptcies?" *Review of Business and Economics*, report that nearly 50% of states have heavy farm influence.

[70] Tiffany O'Callaghan, "Diabetes Expected to Double, Costs to Triple in 2034," *Time Healthland*, November 27, 2009.

How Freedoms Reduce Freedom

We live in the land of the free. The Constitution of the United States and the Bill of Rights provide basic freedoms to all citizens. Among these are freedom of speech, freedom to gather, freedom of religion, freedom to receive equal protection and freedom from unreasonable searches and seizures. In exchange for these freedoms we are asked for very little in return: we must pay taxes, we must serve in the armed forces if drafted, and we must obey the laws of the land. By contrast, loyalty, fidelity, and service to the basic ideals for which this country stands are not required of citizens. It is hard to understand why anyone would object to the American system and our way of life. It is harder still to imagine why anyone would want to change it at least in a very fundamental way. But people who want to remove our freedoms do exist and when they are citizens they enjoy the same basic freedoms as everyone else.

The unintended consequence of the freedoms established for all Americans is that people working to undermine our liberty are able to come to this country and once here subvert our way of life. The court system which is the adjudicator of what we can and cannot do generally takes a blind eye to these threats and does not distinguish between a terrorist who wants to destroy America or someone who wants to pray in school. The reason for this myopia is that our constitutional fathers feared the establishment of a system of preferences benefiting one group over another. Their concerns included avoiding the primacy of one religion (e.g., Quakers versus Puritans) or one political party (e.g., Federalist versus Democratic-Republicans). Our laws and customs have strived to create a level playing field for all citizens. Our forefathers had no way to foresee the development of groups such as Al Qaeda whose desire for a world caliphate envisions America as subsumed simply as another Muslim nation.

This unintended consequence is probably the most painful of those described in this book. No one likes to be taken advantage of, and that appears to be what is happening. The American system of freedom was established not because it benefits one group, one religion, or one ideology over others but because it seeks to put all on the same platform with equal treatment. How unfortunate if we have to change our way of life to be able to combat a vicious foe that is willing to die in order to remove our freedoms. Tony Blair's poignant editorial, "Making Muslim Integration Work," should be must reading for everybody in the political arena.[71]

How Good Government Decisions Create Complications

Governments around the world now realize that they are incapable of running businesses well. In the former Soviet Union, China and elsewhere, many state-run enterprises (SREs) have been privatized and converted to equity ownership. Although the process of conversion has not always been equitable, oligarchs in Russia had relationships with governmental power brokers, the results have generally been favorable. Converted SREs have modernized their operations and downsized their workforce and in the process have become competitive.

Sometimes, unfortunately, best intentions lead to unintended consequences. A good example of this occurred in the South American country of Columbia in the city of Buenaventura when the government privatized the city's port. Formerly a major employer in the city the port provided workers with secure jobs, good wages, and generous benefits. Following the port's privatization, the

[71] Tony Blair, "Making Muslim Integration Work, *The Wall Street Journal*, November 10, 2010.

unemployment rate in the city rose to 28%.[72] Rampant unemployment in a city of 300,000 people especially when the city has recently been prosperous can easily lead to no good. Many residents of Buenaventura turned to the drug trade.[73] While those at the top of these illegal activities undoubtedly have prospered, the rest of the city and its residents have suffered. Portions of the city became shantytowns and Buenaventura has Columbia's highest homicide rate: 144 deaths per hundred thousand people.[74]

The negative unintended consequences of privatization activities in Columbia are presumably outweighed by the positive good that comes from getting the government out of business activities. The lesson to take from Buenaventura is that all government decisions need to be run through a do-no-harm check prior to being implemented including programs that are necessary and beneficial. Had that been done in Buenaventura, the energy and creativity of its town folks may have been channeled into legitimate activities.

How Constitutional Protection Becomes Excessive

In 1963 the Supreme Court ruled that it was unfair for a criminal defendant to be unrepresented in court. Soon states, cities, and counties created public defender's offices funded by government and charged with providing pro bono defense to indigent defendants. Few would argue that the scales of justice were fairly balanced before this court ruling and most would applaud its extension of proper legal consul to all regardless of their ability to pay.

---

[72] Simon Romero, "Cocaine Wars turn Port into Columbia's Deadliest City," *The New York Times*, May 22, 2007.
[73] ibid.
[74] ibid.

The question of what constitutes an adequate constitutional defense remains a perplexing issue confronting the public defender system. The issue boils down to how much defense or defense spending is required in order to give a defendant a fair trial. In most locations public defenders can assemble teams of attorneys, hire expert witnesses and apply for training to ensure the adequate defense of a client.[75] While there are many cases where defendants are still inadequately protected for a variety of reasons, other cases exist wherein the scales of justice have swung too far in the other direction.

The twofold unintended consequence of this Supreme Court interpretation of the Constitution is that 1) in some cases excessive money is spent to protect the rights of a small number of indigent defendants and 2) by exhausting public defender funds on a few cases other defendants are poorly represented or have long waits for representation. The case of Brian Nichols illustrates the unintended consequences that arise when controversial or highly publicized cases are handled by the public defender's office. Mr. Nichols while being tried on a rape charge went on a killing rampage beginning in the courthouse where he killed the presiding judge, a court reporter, a sheriff's deputy, and afterwards a US customs agent.[76] After being captured in the home of a kidnapped hostage Nichols was charged with 54 felonies. The public defender's office appointed four attorneys and allowed the retention of expert witnesses creating a total defense cost exceeding $1.5 million dollars. Nichols was found guilty and was sentenced to multiple life sentences.

Everyone deserves an adequate defense; that's what the Supreme Court decision means. Georgia's statewide public defender's system ran out of money partially because

---

[75] Jenny Jarvie, "GA Public Defense Program Overwhelmed," *Boston Sunday Globe*, April 1, 2007.
[76] ibid.

of Brian Nichols' defense. Consequently, 75 capital cases in the state were put on hold until such time as the public defender's office had additional funding.[77] Many people objected to the amount of money spent to defend Mr. Nichols because there were a number of witnesses to these shootings and Mr. Nichols had confessed. No one would argue that he should not have a defense; it is the impact of the unintended consequence of his defense on others that causes concern. Certainly some of the 75 defendants in the other delayed capital cases were innocent but presumably remained incarcerated while the state searched for funds for the public defender's office.

Similar discussions will most certainly arise in the coming decade concerning the cost of government provided medical care. The topic will arise in reference to insurance provided to the uninsured as well as the cost of government-sponsored medical programs such as Medicare and Medicaid. During the debate over ObamaCare, it was proposed that Cadillac plans or gold-plated plans providing the very best medical care should be taxed. The question will arise whether recipients of government paid insurance and healthcare benefits should not also obtain gold-plated healthcare. As always, the debate will have two constituents; those receiving the benefits who for the most part will want the best care possible and those paying for the benefits who will ask why should assistance recipients get better medical assistance than I do?

Is there a functional equivalence between spending $1.5 million to defend a confessed murderer and spending $400,000 on medical care for a 95-year-old person while in the hospital in the last two weeks of his life? These are tough decisions for any society and they are tougher for one whose economy is matured and slow-growing. They invoke the conflict between equity and prudence; we want to do the right thing but how much should we spend to do it? The

---

[77] ibid.

bigger social questions of equity and prudence are beyond the scope of this book. In contrast, the inevitability of unintended consequences when uninhibited social programs are paid for out of the general tax fund is exactly the focal point of this volume. We all want to live in an equitable society that is prudent with its scarce resources. Helping one person in the most generous of fashions and thereby harming others is an unintended consequence that should not be ignored until after the fact. Budgetary decisions, to be equitable, should consider the plight of all the needy and not just the first in line or the one whose case is covered most spectacularly in the news media.

How much can be asked of taxpayers? Endlessly increasing taxes so that society can provide unlimited or gold-plated benefits to indigent or elderly citizens has unintended consequences that need to be considered. Families with less disposable income following a tax increase must necessarily cut back on other worthwhile spending such as healthcare, education, or family time together. It is important for society to balance the benefits of helping those in need against the cost, including the unintended consequence cost, of taxing citizens excessively.

The problem of allocating limited resources to those in need is not confined to the US. Recently, the United Kingdom elected a new government, headed by David Cameron, a member of the conservative party. Cameron was appointed Prime Minister in May of 2010. Describing himself as a liberal conservative, Cameron has set out to reshape the British landscape. Among the changes proposed for England include a radical reduction in the legal aid system.

The legal aid system in the UK has a $3.4 billion budget; Cameron intends to reduce that by $560 million. Currently, the system pays legal expenses for both civil and criminal cases. Cameron will save this money by halting government assistance in civil cases. Justice Minister, Kenneth Clarke, said they want to "discourage people from resorting to lawyers whenever they face a problem."[78] Mr. Clarke seems to be saying that an unintended consequence of the current system is that people with grievances depend on the courts rather than having a conversation. Whenever a government allocates money to a specific need, people recognize the signal and alter their behavior to accommodate government funding for activities that previously were paid for individually.

Some lawyers in the UK working with the legal aid system earn as it is much as $1.6 million a year.[79] There is nothing wrong with anyone earning any amount of money; the problem is that if the government was not footing the bill these lawyers would be earning far less. People are taking advantage of the system. David Cameron is saying that there are limits to how much money a government should spend to enable the less fortunate to behave like their more wealthy litigious peers.

How Protecting Highways Endangers People

Economic forces oblige truckers to use larger and heavier rigs as they seek a competitive advantage in the distribution of goods. Heavier trucks more quickly damage highways and bridges and may pose a greater danger to automobile traffic. To protect and preserve the nation's highways the US Department of Transportation (DOT) Federal Highway Administration regulates the industry using powers given to it by the Federal-Aid Highway Act of 1956. DOT'S regulations include size and weight standards that it imposes on the trucking fleet.

---

[78] John F Burns," British Premiere Plans Deep Cuts in Aid for Civil Litigants," *The New York Times*, November 15, 2010.
[79] ibid.

Currently the federal limit on trucks size is 80,000 pounds.[80] Industry advocates have suggested raising the weight limit to 100,000 pounds. Detractors, such as Jackie Gillan of the special interest group Advocates for Highway and Auto Safety argue that after seeing a major bridge collapse in Minneapolis in 2007 that the current weight standard is sufficient.[81] The International Brotherhood of Teamsters, a powerful truckers union, also opposes the idea since it would result in a reduction in the demand for truckers.[82] In 2010 the DOT permitted, on an experimental basis, the use of larger trucks in two states: Maine and Vermont.

For the most part everyone is ignoring the unintended consequence of requiring smaller trucks. These unintended consequences arise because the DOT is only empowered to regulate federal roads; state transportation agencies regulate state roads. In Maine for example, the state agency permits larger rigs to ride on state roads. Here is where the unintended consequence arises. Truckers when permitted by state regulation use larger rigs on state roads which are often just two lanes wide. When the DOT limits the use of big rigs on federal roads truckers owning these vehicles simply move, whenever possible, to state roads. The dangers present when large trucks use four lane roads is presumably far less than when those same trucks use smaller highways.

State highways often run through villages and communities with small populations. When a convoy of larger trucks barrels down a state road, buildings shake and people quake. During the one-year pilot program in Maine and Vermont, larger rigs moved off of the state roads and

---

[80] Josh Mitchell, "Truckers Increase Call to Pull Heavier Loads on Highways," *The Wall Street Journal*, November 22, 2010.
[81] ibid.
[82] ibid.

onto the Interstate.[83] Not only was life more pleasant for people whose lives were no longer disrupted by the larger rigs but it is likely that there were fewer traffic fatalities with larger rigs using the interstate rather than smaller state roads. The unintended consequence of possibly doing the right thing to protect the integrity of highways may have been the loss of human lives.

How Government is Like the Gang That Couldn't Shoot Straight

The Obama administration passed a health care overhaul in 2010. The repudiation by the electorate of President Obama in November 2010 in part relates to health care legislation. ObamaCare, as it is colloquially known, is designed to reduce the number of uninsured Americans thereby helping hospitals to cover the cost of administering health care to uninsured patients. Whether ObamaCare is a good idea or not, hospitals should not have higher bills to pay post passage of ObamaCare.

An unintended consequence of this new legislation is that it ended what had been called the 340 B program which is a pseudonym derived from the applicable numbered section of the Public Health Service Act of 1944. Section 340 B mandated that drug manufacturers give certain healthcare providers discounts ranging up to 50%.[84] With the passage of ObamaCare ended the portion of 340 B that applied discounts to orphan drugs (affecting fewer than 200,000 people) purchased by children's hospitals. The unintended consequence of ObamaCare is the loss of this discount. Without the discount, children's hospitals annually pay

---

[83] ibid.
[84] Robert Pear, "Wrinkle in New Health Law Cost Children's Hospitals Discounts on Some Drugs," *The New York Times*, December 8, 2010.

hundreds of millions of dollars more than they paid prior to the passage of ObamaCare. [85]

How Even Simple Governmental Restrictions have Consequences

Who would think that there would be unintended consequences from telling a kid to wear a helmet when riding a bicycle? A recent article in the *Journal of Law and Economics* by Christopher S. Carpenter and Mark F Stehr[86] analyzed states which had recently enacted helmet laws. They found across the 21 states falling into that category and in the District of Columbia that there was a 19% reduction in fatalities in the 5 - 15 age category after a state mandates the use of bicycle helmets. Carpenter and Stehr surveyed parents to determine why the drop in accidents occurred. The obvious answer was that the kids began wearing bicycle helmets while riding their bikes; but the surprising result was that after state enacted helmet legislation about 650,000 fewer kids rode their bikes each year. The reported success of fewer fatalities could have been similarly achieved if these states had outlawed bicycle riding altogether.

Virginia Postrel called this response "a dork affect." [87] She argues that kids would rather walk than ride a bike while wearing a helmet for fear of being called a dork or worse by their peers. According to her calculations, for each life saved by a bicycle helmet 81,000 fewer kids rode bikes. It would be easy to say that imposing this law was worthwhile since

---

[85] Ibid.

[86] Christopher S. Carpenter and Mark F Stehr, "Intended and Unintended Effects of Youth Bicycle Helmet Laws," *National Bureau of Economic Research Paper No. 15658,* January 2010.

[87] Virginia Postrel, "The Bike Helmet War", *The Wall Street Journal*, October 9, 2010.

every life is worth saving even though just eight bicycle accident fatalities occur annually on average in the age 5 - 15 age category. After all, eight lives are eight lives. But that simplistic view ignores the unintended consequences of legislation.

Some of the 650,000 kids walking to school or the mall rather than commuting by bicycle were probably injured or even killed in another form of accident, perhaps with a car, a bus or a truck. Those accidental deaths are not balanced against the lives saved by helmets because it is unknown whether the children would have been on bicycles if they could have ridden them without helmets. Moreover, some children may have been injured while riding in cars driven by friends (both under aged and those with legal driver's licenses) or parents.

How do statisticians account for the impact of kids no longer riding bicycles on the plague of childhood obesity? How many non-bike riders will suffer from early onset diabetes, cardiovascular disease, or other ailments as a consequence of their trying not to be a dork?

How Even Simple Governmental Restrictions have Consequences: Part 2

A growing number of municipalities including Los Angeles, Fairfax County, and others have banned the consumption of chocolate milk when students eat at schools. On its face, the ban makes sense given the sugar content of chocolate milk. Well-meaning parents and educators no doubt assumed that children kept from drinking chocolate milk would turn instead to regular milk. Unfortunately, the data does not support that hypothesis. For example, the Milk Processors Education Program reports that milk consumption declined by 35% in schools banning chocolate milk. [88] Similarly a report in the *Washington Post* indicates

---

[88] Barb N., "Chocolate Milk Ban in Schools Impacts Kids Milk Consumption,"

that milk consumption declines by 37% when flavored milk is removed. [89] Apparently children reach for soda or sports drinks when their chocolate milk is removed. If only water and regular milk were the available alternatives the ban on chocolate milk might have worked. Hence, the report of lower consumption of milk appears in equal parts to be a result of poorly conceived government regulations and government efforts to regulate food consumption.

How Horses, Dogs and Unions Eat Themselves to Death

A vivid scene in the 1971 Jan Troell movie *The Emigrants* occurs when a young daughter, who like the rest of her family has had too little to eat for months, dies after gorging on a hidden cache of grain. Unlike the 1973 film by Marco Ferreri, *La Grande Bouffe*, in which a group of men retire to a beautiful villa that they have filled with the finest food and drink and set about eating themselves to death, most victims of overindulgence are more like the daughter in *The Emigrants*: they do not realize how their actions ultimately will lead to their own demise.

Starting in 1932, during the Great Depression, Congress passed initiatives that transferred power in labor negotiations from management to workers. The first of these was the Norris-LaGuardia Act of 1932 which restrained the use of injunctions against striking unions. The election of President Franklin Delano Roosevelt in the following year encouraged the notion of collective bargaining as being a right. In June 1933 workers received the right to organize into unions with the passage of the National Industrial

---

http://business.gather.com/viewArticle.action?articleId=28147497931 6349, obtained on July 20, 2011.
[89] Jen Singer, "The Unwise War Against Chocolate Milk," *The Wall Street Journal*, April 19, 2011.

Recovery Act[90] which after being struck down by a Supreme Court ruling was replaced by the corrected Wagner Act of 1935. Some argue that these laws create labor cartels which in some instances forces workers who want to work to join unions.[91]

Ultimately in manufacturing industries the balance between labor and management shifted so that labor unions gained the upper hand. For years, the United Auto Workers (UAW) played off one of the big three automakers, usually starting with the weakest, against the other two to establish a standard contract, often with new and expensive provisions. Similar processes were applied in other sectors of the economy as well including steel, grocery stores, and newspapers.[92]

Before unions obtained government sanctioned rights there was not much of a middle class in America.[93] By the mid-1950s, the middle-class had become a significant component of the economy. In fact, in 1951 the sociologist C. Wright Mills wrote *White Collar: The American Middle Classes* the first major study of the middle-class in the US. Since then the middle-class has been thought to be comprised of two groups: a higher paid group of well-educated workers and a lower paid echelon of skilled craftsmen and unionized workers.

Economic development in the past half-century has promoted the quantity of education offered and taken.

---

[90] Russell O Wright, *Chronology of Labor in the United States,* McFarland and Company, Inc., Publishers, 2003.

[91] Holman W Jenkins Jr.,"Obama's Last Stand in the Air," *The Wall Street Journal*, September 15, 2010.

[92] Ibid.

[93] Labor economists, including the author, have demonstrated that nonunion workers during strong economic periods receive comparable wage and salary increases as their unionized peers. Many argue that unions only create a wage differential during slack economic times.

According to the Current Population Survey and the 1950 Census of the Population the proportion of Americans receiving college degrees at the Bachelor's level rose from 5% in 1947 to nearly 30% today. Over the same period, the proportion of the population with a high school diploma rose from roughly 33% to nearly 85%. Presumably, more workers have entered the middle-class as a result of their acquisition of human capital rather than entering the middle-class as a result of unions. The need for unions by industrial and service workers, though still present, is far less than it had been during the Great Depression.

Over time, labor unions won a decent wage and then generous wages and benefits for their members. The unintended consequence of the legislation enabling union activities has been the creation of a cost structure which makes some industries unsustainable. In those cases, jobs either move to nonunion regions, for example steel to the south or they move offshore, for example the automotive sector. It was estimated that in 2008 the average UAW worker received $70 per hour all in including pensions and benefits.[94] For a 2,000 hour work year that amounts to approximately $140,000 annually. According to the International Monetary Fund, the average compensation of all workers in the US is approximately $46,000 a year[95]. The nearly $100,000 annual differential paid to UAW members is approximately 200% over and above the base or normal salary in America. While it is arguable that the skills required to work at an auto assembly plant are somewhat higher than the skills required working at the average job in the US, it is highly doubtful that a 200% premium is required to attract a sufficient number of workers.

---

[94] Andrew Ross Sorkin," A Bridge Loan? US Should Guide GM in a Chapter 11," *The New York Times*, November 17, 2008.
[95] *World Economic Outlook Database,* 2010, International Monetary Fund, October.

Prior to the giant wave of unionization the proportion of funds allocated to labor (and not to capital) was probably too low. In 1928 for example labor received approximately 67% of the value of the nation's output. This increased gradually (ignoring a dramatic blip during the height of the Depression when profits became negative) until it reached a peak in 1974 of a little more than 73% of the total value of the economy's output.[96] Since then the number has declined slightly.

Making rules that are too one-sided creates during a negotiation inevitability regarding who will be the ultimate winner. Recently, the Obama administration's National Mediation Board (NMB) has moved to change how votes are counted in union elections.[97] For 75 years employees who did not vote had their ballots counted as no votes. To create what the NMB describes as a more democratic election process starting in July 2010 votes will be counted only using ballots that have been cast. That is, a vote not cast is a vote not counted. In the first major unionization vote since the adoption of the new rules, gate and reservation agents at Delta Airlines Inc. voted down the union for the third time with 8,700 workers voting against the union versus 3,600 voting in favor of the union. Over 3,000 workers chose not to vote. After seeing the harm brought on industries such as automotive and steel by the unintended consequence of having a wage structure that is too high, it is unfortunate that the Obama administration adopted this new rule.

---

[96] Paul Gomme and Peter Rupert, "Measuring Labor's Share of Income," Federal Reserve Bank of Cleveland, Policy Discussion Papers, Number 7, November, 2004.
[97] Op Cit, Jenkins.

How Central Planning Invariably Gets It Wrong

The great debate between Frederick Hayek and John Maynard Keynes on the subject of free markets versus central planning continues to this day. Writing during a period of slack economic demand, the Great Depression, those economists had different views on the ability of free markets to adjust to circumstances and create sufficient demands to reemploy the population. Keynes was a principal advocate of government spending and advised governments in both the US and UK. Hayek who was awarded the Nobel Prize in economics in 1974 profoundly believed that socialist or collectivist thought would result in *The Road to Serfdom* which was the title of his famous polemic on the topic.

The question of whether the free market produces better results than central planning remains unanswered. The Soviet Union has moved away from a purely communist economic model. The Chinese have permitted a move towards grassroots capitalism. This book cannot address the critical Keynes/Hayek question directly but what it will do is to point out the unintended consequences of central planning.

Everyone in the world is familiar with the terrible famine that has ravaged Ethiopia. What is less well known is how central planning contributed to this disaster. The tale begins in the 1970s when the Derg, a communist military junta, fought against Emperor Haile Selassie I of Ethiopia (he ruled from 1930 through 1974). Famine was not unknown in Ethiopia before the Derg. They however initiated a policy of relocation which moved people to southern Ethiopia away from an opposing rebel group. Alex de Waal, a noted aid write is quoted in a *Wall Street Journal* book review saying, "Resettlement certainly killed people at a faster rate than the famine. "[98] During Ethiopia's infamous 1984 famine, the Derg made an even greater central planning blunder. They issued an order requiring farmers to sell their crops at low prices to the government.[99] Not reckoning with the powerful forces of unintended consequences, the policy was subterfuged when farmers ate what they had grown rather than sell it to the Government. The central planners forgot that people behave in their own best interest. With the grain eaten, none was planted the next year. Self-interest led to an unintended consequence and to a worsening of the famine.

Interestingly, Hayek believed that government decisions often produced unintended consequences.[100] Ronald Reagan adopted this view. Sadly too few modern politicians have accepted this starkly simple idea.

How Unlike Old Soldiers Government Largess Never Fades Away

Congress hears that money is needed for some urgent purpose, facts are presented to support the need, and after a sufficient amount of horse-trading between political parties, regions of the country, and individual politicians funding is approved. Congress may start out appropriating a small amount of money but over time as the program continues and as funding gradually escalates, a monster is created. Do this for 70 years and you have the recipe for an insupportable government budget.

While the power of compounding explains a portion of business success, for example in real estate, the principle when applied to government creates a debacle. A small leak

---

[98] William Easterly, "The Hazards of Doing Good," *The Wall Street Journal*, September 7, 2010.
[99] Ibid.
[100] Francis Fukuyama, "Big Government Skeptic," *The New York Times Sunday Book Review*, May 8, 2011

becomes a flood as potentially unnecessary expenditures persist year after year with growing appropriations. Michael J Boskin the former head of the Council of Economic Advisers under President Bush notes that the federal government decided in the 1970s after virtually no analysis to index Social Security benefits to wage inflation rather than price inflation. [101] Wage inflation normally exceeds price inflation. The decision created trillions of dollars of additional unfunded Social Security benefits. Boskin quotes Albert Einstein to have said "compound interest is the most powerful force in the universe." The unintended consequence of small government appropriations (chestnuts) is that they grow into huge oak trees.

In addition to the two questions asked earlier in this chapter, two questions need to be asked before allocating government money: 1) is the government responsible for or the appropriate party to provide a remedy for this "apparent" problem, and 2) if the answer to the first question is yes, when do government payments stop? The unintended consequence of a generous government and a political system which passes laws by horse-trading is described by combining the immortal words of General Douglas MacArthur and the famous Eveready battery commercial, "old government programs don't die they just keep on spending."

Outside of Johnston Pennsylvania sits the airport to nowhere. [102] Officially it is called the John Murtha Johnstown-Cambria County Airport. On a good day the airport might have three flights each of which carries 10 passengers. As these 30 passengers arrive at the airport they are screened by TSA employees using expensive high tech security apparatus, can eat at a fancy restaurant, and depart

---

[101] Michael J Boskin, "Five Lessons for Deficit Busters," *The Wall Street Journal*, June 20, 2011.
[102] Ron Nixon, "Politics Gives Some US Subsidy Programs Staying Power," *The New York Times*, July 15, 2011, A 16.

on a modern runway. Unless these passengers are rock stars or oil barons no airport could survive with so few passengers. However, in 1978 Congress passed the Essential Air Services program to supply air service in regions where no airline making a business decision would otherwise fly. As of 2011 the program applied to 152 communities. Its original $7 annual million funding is now $200 million. The subsidy at the John Murtha Airport is $1.6 million a year or about $150 per passenger. Some of the 152 airports have subsidies in excess of $1,000 per passenger. In many cases, alternative airports are within a two hour car ride.

If the Essential Air Services program was the only example of an undying and apparently unnecessary program the US budget deficit would not be a problem. Unfortunately, there are hundreds or perhaps thousands of such programs. Compounding the problem are turf wars fought between government agencies resulting in needless duplication. For example, the Government Accounting Office reports that over 50 government agencies supervise programs to help the homeless. [103] Is homelessness a problem? Of course it is. Does the federal government need so much duplication? Of course it doesn't. But the remedy of shutting down an agency or reducing employment in the federal government is an anathema to our system.

Government money is no different than cookies in a cookie jar. When there are no limits placed on the consumption of cookies the cookie jar is soon empty. Some parents limit their kids to one or two cookies a day and in that way always have some cookies in the jar. A balanced budget amendment would serve just such a purpose. It would say to the profligate spenders this is how much money we have and this is how much you can spend. As in the example of a family and its cookie jar, if everyone in a family

[103] Government Accounting Office, Homelessness: Improving Program Coordination and Client Access to Programs, statement of Stanley J Czerwinski, March 6, 2002.

of five knows that each week the cookie jar is replenished with 35 cookies then it is clear that each person can have one cookie per day. If government operated with a balanced budget then rather than funding every cause, problem, and opportunity the government would prioritize its needs and stop funding the rest.

How Corporate Average Fuel Economy (CAFE) Changed More Than Fuel Economy

America is too dependent on foreign sources of energy. No one would disagree. On the other hand, nobody agrees on how to change things. Markets work when consumer decisions respond to price levels. When chicken is cheaper than steak, all other things held equal, more chicken is purchased at the supermarket than steak. The same "radical" solution to the energy problem, through higher taxes, has never been tried; the influence of special interest groups may explain why. Instead, Congress tries to solve the problem using regulation.

One piece of the legislative pie passed in 1975 is The Corporate Average Fuel Economy (CAFE). CAFE imposes a sales weighted average fuel economy standard on auto manufacturers encompassing all vehicles for sale in the US weighing less than 8,500 pounds. A definitive study of the impact of CAFE conducted by the national Academy of science estimated a 14% reduction in fuel consumption. [104] On the surface, the regulations achieved what they set out to accomplish.

---

[104] Board On Energy and Environmental Systems,. *Effectiveness and Impact of Corporate Average Fuel Economy (CAFE) Standards (2002)*, The National Academies.

Few government regulations are free of unintended consequences. The CAFE program is no exception. CAFE caused the demise of the family station wagon. Political dickering substituted a more lax fuel economy standard for light trucks. The initial regulations classified minivans as light trucks and not cars. Auto manufacturers figured out that they could sell more low mileage vehicles by replacing station wagons with minivans. Arguably minivans have many advantages over station wagons, though the reverse is also true. The movement away from station wagons was not consumer-based but driven by regulation.

The National Academy of Sciences report detailed a more deadly unintended consequence of CAFE. It suggested that there were as many as 2,600 additional fatalities annually as a result of the transition away from station wagons. Minivans have a higher center of gravity then do automobiles making them more prone to rollovers; the same is true for SUVs which more recently were classified as light trucks. Among the objectionable aspects of these deaths is that they occurred because fuel economy regulations made the family station wagon a dinosaur while encouraging minivans use. Had people switched from station wagons to a more dangerous vehicle type as a reaction to higher prices driven by tax increases, the choice would have been theirs: lower cost and less safety. But these deaths came not from choice but from an unintended consequence.

How the Alternative Minimum Tax (AMT) Ensnares Innocent Taxpayers

The AMT was enacted in 1969. Its purpose was simple: to ensure that all taxpayers paid at least a minimum tax. It was referred to as the Millionaire's Tax. Numerous tax loopholes enabled the wealthiest to pay no tax at all. For example, a single dollar invested in oil and gas wells provided tax write-offs in excess of a dollar. A reformatted AMT was enacted in 1982 but like its predecessor it ignored inflation. As nominal income levels (not real) rise, more Americans are caught in the AMT trap. In 2010 AMT kicked in at an income level of $87,500 for both trusts and married people living separately; singles and those married individuals filing jointly hit AMT level at $175,000. Once again the power of compounding rears its ugly head: why else treat $87,500 like a million dollars?

The AMT has a very complicated formula but basically it takes away personal exemptions and standard deductions. AMT causes middle income Americans to pay higher taxes. The unintended consequence of Congress's efforts to get all Americans to pay some taxes is that middle income Americans pay more tax than they should. It is estimated that Americans pay more than $100 billion a year in incremental taxes because of the AMT.

How Politically Correct Decisions Make Bad Choices

Political correctness (PC) occurs when it is more important to mollify the feelings of a minority group than it is to make the right decision, say the right thing, or even express certain ideas. How to control PC behavior is not the subject of this book. Instead this section concerns the unintended consequence of a city doing its business following a PC agenda.

In 2010 the city of Los Angeles finished construction on the Robert F Kennedy Community Schools Complex at a cost of $578 million. The school is designed to educate 4,260 students. The cost per seat is approximately $136,000. At a time when both the state of California and the City of Los Angeles are suffering from financial shortfalls the expenditure stands out like a football in church. During the previous two years, the city laid off 3,000 teachers as it tried to combat a $640 million deficit. [105]

Thomas Rubin, a consultant to the Los Angeles Unified School District tasked with overseeing the bonds issued to pay for this and other newly constructed schools, in an interview remarked that it was "a tremendous screw-up" that "should have been studied closer beforehand."[106] Allysha Findley notes that the project had been abandoned only to resurface again "after community activist demanded that the school be built at whatever cost necessary in order to show respect for the neighborhood's Latino children."[107] In other words, PC comes first, rational analysis second. Could the project have come in less expensively? There is no doubt of that. For example, the price tag included $1.3 million for murals and artwork: probably an unnecessary expenditure.

Should towns build new schools when the old ones are overcrowded and outdated? Of course they should. But should they consider alternative mechanisms to deliver the education to children? Of course they should again.

Charter schools in the Los Angeles Unified School District built to accommodate 4,260 students have cost less than $85 million to build. [108] Charter schools in Los Angeles have nearly twice the graduation rate of regular schools. So the equation looked like this then: Choice 1 - be PC and build an expensive school with a low graduation rate or Choice 2 - build a cheaper school which graduates nearly twice as many students. Unfortunately, the powers of PC outweighed proper thinking and Choice 1 was taken. The unintended

---

[105] Associated Press, *Sacramento Bee*, August 22, 2010.
[106] Allysha Finley, "Broke-in Building the Most Expensive School in US History," *The Wall Street Journal*, September 4, 2010.
[107] Ibid.
[108] Ibid.

consequence of being PC is a financially destitute city which has failed to conduct its educational mission for children.

How You Shouldn't Wish For Things

The adage that you shouldn't wish for things because you might get them was probably written by someone concerned about unintended consequences. That's what happened in New York City after the State passed a law making it illegal for owners of rental buildings to use them as short-term hotels. As discussed above in, How Price Controls Hurt Intended Beneficiaries, New York City suffers under a variety of rent-limiting programs. As a result of limitations on apartment rents, landlords converted apartments into hotel rooms. [109] If a landlord cannot make a profit renting a rent-controlled apartment and if the state will not let it be used as a hotel room then it's not surprising when landlords do something else.

The unintended consequence of these restrictions on landlords is that some of them began to use their property as homeless shelters. [110] Imagine how upset neighbors were when they discovered that the solution to the problem they thought they had, a law preventing the rental of apartments as hotel rooms, had an unintended consequence which many of them perceived as far worse: moving a homeless shelter into their neighborhood.

How It Must be Easier to Herd Cats

In a famous scene in Jean-Luc Godard's film *Week End* there is an endless traffic jam of cars leaving Paris. A similar scene occurs in the recent Spielberg version of *War of the*

---

[109] Cara Buckley, "Law on Apartments as Hotel Rooms has Unintended Effect," *The New York Times*, January 14, 2011.
[110] Ibid.

Worlds. For Godard the scene attacks bourgeoisie life; for Spielberg the message was simpler, it's not easy moving thousands or millions of people at the same time. What should a government do in the face of a disaster, natural or otherwise? The recent nuclear meltdown in Japan is an example of a situation requiring mass evacuation. Hurricanes in the Gulf of Mexico and flooding along major rivers are other examples.

Most cities, towns and nuclear power stations have large scale evacuation plans that can be effectuated in the case of emergency. A problem with these plans is that it is difficult to test them; that is, it is doubtful, for example, that all the citizens of Chattanooga Tennessee would agree to pretend to evacuate the city on some Tuesday at 1:30. Instead, planners rely on historical experiences, most likely in other locations, and on logical assessments to craft the best evacuation plans possible.

The unintended consequent of trying to evacuate large numbers of people and their animals at the same time is that mishaps occur. For example, in 2005 when Hurricane Rita approached the city of Houston along the Gulf Coast the mayor, hoping to avoid the disaster that had afflicted New Orleans, ordered the mass evacuation of the city. In short order interstates around the city ground to a standstill and many people spent days in their car.[111] There were more deaths and injuries as a result of the evacuation than from the storm itself.

The lessons learned from this experience are that populations need to be bifurcated into those most at risk and those at less risk. Evacuating people most at risk, while leaving those in less risk in their homes, creates a more orderly evacuation - provided that those at less risk do not panic and join the others.

---

[111] Gardiner Harris, "Dangers of Leaving No Resident Behind," *The New York Times*, March 22, 2011.

How Trying to Protect Someone May Bring Them Harm

A well-functioning securities market requires that the playing field be level between investors. That said, someone willing to work harder or dig deeper can create for themselves a natural investing advantage. Someone once said about investing that it is a knowledge game; whoever has the most knowledge wins the game. Some investors unable to legitimately create an edge for themselves seek an easier, albeit illegal, avenue to success - they cheat. The easiest and most surefire way to gain an unfair advantage is by trading with inside information.

Insider trading is defined as decision-making based on nonpublic information. There is a long history in the US of efforts to control and combat insider trading. In 2000, the SEC promulgated Regulation Fair Disclosure (FD) which restricted company insiders from selectively distributing information. [112] Prior to FD, companies might divulge information to key mutual fund managers in an effort to curry their support and interest in the company. After FD, all nonpublic information must be released at the same time to all investors.

An unintended consequence of this regulation was created by the existence of a loophole not dealt with by Regulation FD: mid-level executives were assumed to not know critical information. A market was created which matched mid-level executives, described as experts, with investors willing to pay for that knowledge. Experts were paid as much as $1,000 an hour. Even after the public

---

[112] Gregory Zuckerman and Susan Pulliam, "How an SEC Crackdown Led to Rise of Expert Networks," *The Wall Street Journal*, December 17, 2010.

development of this marketplace no one at the SEC proposed to shut the loophole. [113]

The companies which worked as matchmakers between hedge funds and mid-level executives had "policies" which required that improper nonpublic information not be shared. Without improper information being transferred to the investors, the mid-level executives had no value. The matchmaker's policy is akin to a passage in a life insurance policy that says the policy is voided if one were to die: it makes no sense. Yet when a number of mid-level executives were arrested for insider trading in 2010 the companies which matched them with investors pointed their fingers at those arrested and vehemently argued they themselves had done nothing wrong.

Some financial market experts such as Milton Friedman and Thomas Sowell argue that insider trading laws/regulations should be removed. Among the arguments for such actions are that it would allow financial markets to react to events and information sooner. Others note the absence of similar regulations in real estate transactions, where the information available to the buyer and seller are unequal. Readers of this book might have a third argument against insider trading regulations: no regulation is sufficiently robust to exclude ambiguities that lead to loopholes that can be circumvented thereby enabling some people to take advantage of situations while the general investor is led to believe, by the existence of the laws, that this is never the case.

---

[113] Ibid.

BRUNNER BRIDGE AND COAL MINES, GREY VALLEY NZ 178 JK

Chapter 3

Human Inspired Unintended Consequences

How Human Error Causes Environmental Damage

During the summer of 2010 Russia was plagued by an almost impenetrable smoke barrier arising from peat bog fires. Over 1,000 peat bog fires were reported that summer. The probable cause of the unquenchable fires was a decision made in the pre 1920s to drain swamps so that peat could be mined as a fuel for electric power plants. The practice continued for four decades until peat was replaced by Siberian natural gas. The current problems might have been avoided if the peat swamps had been reflooded. But they weren't. The unintended consequence of an economic decision in 1920 has created a modern health risk.

Unlike forest fires in which noxious smoke rises high into the atmosphere, smoke from low temperature peat fires hugs the earth and poses special health risks. Unlike forest fires which burn quickly, peat fires burn slowly and they consume up to 10 times the biomass of a forest fire. The Russians have discovered that even after pumping water endlessly onto the fires that they continue as subterranean burns. [114]

People's demand for energy is nearly unquenchable. In the electricity arena, whether the source of the power is hydro, nuclear, or fossil fuel, environmental damages are always a danger. Hydroelectric dams divert rivers and inhibit the migratory path of fish; nuclear plants over and above their radiation risks require massive water cooling from standing bodies of water such as lakes or oceans thereby raising water temperatures; and fossil fuel based electricity production emits carbon dioxide, particulates, and heavy metals. Solar and wind power which are in their infancy on the surface would seem to be environmentally green but they are likely to have plenty of their own unintended consequences.

How a Puritanical Sexual Ethos Winnows the Political Field

I hope that most of the examples presented in this book are straightforward enough that every reader agrees with their basic facts. The unintended consequence described in this section may not pass that test for every reader. If you find its arguments flawed I hope you will just go on and read the next section.

---

[114] For further reading please see Andrew E. Kramer, "As Russia's Peat Fires Burn on Fingers Point to Mistakes of the Past," *The New York Times*, August 13, 2010.

The pantheon of great presidents and senior politicians seems to have diminished over the last half century. The era of an America with superb politicians like George Washington, Abraham Lincoln, or Ronald Reagan is a thing of the past. Today's political ranks contain the mediocre, the ill informed, and the indolent. There are a number of explanations for why this has occurred but here is another one.

Two common threads unite politicians like Bill Clinton, Eliot Spitzer, Dominique Strauss-Kahn, Mark Sanford, and Strom Thurmond among others: they were excellent politicians who became embroiled in sexual scandals. Other countries in the world, most notably France, ignore the personal side of politicians' lives. As a consequence, the ranks of French politicians are not thinned by a puritanical ethos. In the US on the other hand, it seems that the press devotes more space to sexual scandals than to a discussion of real substantive issues. One question that always emerges is "why somebody would risk so much for what can be perceived as so little?" The common answer is that these politicians are narcissists: someone who is egotistical, vain, or selfish.

A recent article in the journal *Personality and Social Psychology Bulletin* suggests that a mixture of people with personality types combining narcissists with non narcissists creates a dynamic environment in which creativity flourishes.[115] Accepting the conclusions of this article, it may be the case that certain politicians are both egotistical and more creative than average. Their egotism pushes them to engage in sexual misconduct (defined by the puritanical ethos) while their creativity makes them good leaders. When these individuals step over the line and participate in a

---

[115]See "Are two Narcissists Better Than One?: The Link Between Narcissism, Perceived Creativity and Creative Performance", Jack Goncalo, Frances J. Flynn, Sharon H. Kim, *Personality and Social Psychology Bulletin*, 36, 2010, Sage Publications.

sexual activity that becomes fodder for journalist they are forced to resign or otherwise move out of public life. In so doing the rest of us are stripped of a capable leader with a creative vision who might have assisted in the formation of a good policy in order to sell a few extra newspapers.

Spouses of philandering politicians sometimes understand that their narcissistic husbands need to behave in a most unconventional manner. For example, Anne Sinclair, the wife of Dominique Strauss-Kahn replied to a question about her husband in a 2006 interview in *L'Express* a French publication, "No! I'm even proud of it. It's important to seduce, for a politician, as long as he is still attracted to me, and I to him it is sufficient."

For some reason the American public, its journalist and politicians have acquiesced to Puritanism as a "sine qua non" of political life. Anyone who steps over the line is to be outed and then banished. The unintended consequence of adopting these sexual mores, perhaps better suited for the 1700s than for today, is that some of our best potential leaders either permanently shirk public life or are eternally damned after they get booted out of the political spectrum.

Who suffers? If a less creative cadre of politicians remains after the field is winnowed down by removing the most creative, and yes the most egotistical members of the group, then all of us suffer. Perhaps this is the one lesson we should learn from the French.

How Performance Suffers When Sexual Addicts are Outed

Eldrick Tont Woods, otherwise known as Tiger Woods, is without question the greatest golfer the sport has ever had. In 2010 alone, he earned $90.5 million from the combination of tournament play and endorsements. [116] He has won 14 major golf championships and 71 Professional Golfers Association tour events. No other golfer has ever won all the major championships in a single year, the Grand Slam, at such a young age as did Tiger Woods. There has never been another golfer like him.

In 2009 Tiger Woods' marital infidelity surfaced. Following a denied extramarital affair story in the *National Enquirer*, Tiger Woods had a single vehicle car accident early in the morning of November 25, 2009. A media frenzy ensued and eventually at least a dozen women claimed to have had affairs with him. In February 2010 Woods apologized in a nationally televised speech where he revealed that he had gone through therapy, apparently for sexual addiction, but this was not enough and his marriage ended in divorce in August 2010.

After a hiatus, Tiger Woods returned to professional golf in April of 2010. He had been away from the sport for 20 weeks. During the golf season which ended in November of 2010, Tiger Woods had no victories. This was a dramatic change from his success in the previous few years. In 2005, he had six tournament wins and $10.9 million in earnings; he won eight tournaments in 2006 and earned $9.9 million; 2007 followed with seven tournament wins and $10.9 million in earnings; 2008 saw Tiger Woods winning four tournaments and nearly $6 million; and then in 2009 he won six tournaments and $10.5 million. In 2010, Tiger Woods won no tournaments and earned a measly [sic] $1.3 million.

Tiger Woods' unintended consequence was that his performance on the golf course went from being super-human to merely being very good. Possibly, Tiger Woods

---

[116] "Tiger Woods Stays Top of Sport Earnings List". BBC News. July 21, 2010, http://news.bbc.co.uk/sport2/hi/front_page/8843371.stm.

relied upon his wife and the stability of their marriage as an anchor which helped him direct his energies on the golf course; the shattering of that bond may have affected his athletic prowess. Alternatively, he was buried by an avalanche of journalistic overzealousness, with his every move and utterance recorded and transmitted to the nation; the glare from the publicity may have diminished his confidence. Which of these two explanations is correct doesn't matter. What matters, is that the greatest golfer who ever lived has lost his Mojo as an unintended consequence of having been a sexual addict. Had he been more discreet his extraordinary golf course performance may have continued until the end of a long and illustrious career.

How Parental Control Harms Kids

Every parent's nightmare descended upon four families in Leicester Massachusetts late one night in April 2007. [117] Four friends all teenagers died that evening when the car one of them was driving collided with a tree killing four of five passengers. Despite wearing their seat belts all four died instantly. They had been out for a late dinner and were hurrying home racing against a midnight curfew.

It is hard to fault a parent who tells their child to be home at a certain hour. The world is filled with scary things and adolescents suffer from a lack of experience, a sense of immortality, and an almost unnatural interest in determining their own limits. Curfews, especially those with harsh penalties, may force teenagers to risk life and limb in order to satisfy an almost arbitrary parental dictate. Congressman Ron Paul, a libertarian, stated that he had never given his children strict [underlining added by the author] curfews in

---

[117] Scott Allen, "Four Teens are Killed in Leicester Car Crash", *Boston Globe*, April 22, 2007.

fear of the unintended consequence of their speeding home to beat the clock.[118]

Should fear of unintended consequences keep parents from controlling their children? Of course not! Instead, parents need to establish rules to govern conduct and behavior which they enforce selectively and with care. Every rule should be explained carefully so that the child understands why it is important. A strict midnight curfew can be supplanted by a strong recommendation to be home by midnight; failure or better yet repeated failure to follow the suggestion would result in a serious family conversation which might allow the child to reasonably explain why the curfew cannot be adhered to or might result in a slightly modified curfew time. Maybe the best rule is not a rule at all but is rather to lead by example; don't tell your children not to smoke or drink and then smoke or drink yourself, don't tell your children not to use drugs and then abuse them yourself, etc. Maybe the Paul family philosophy should be tried by more families: tell your children to behave themselves and be polite, that's all.

How Cigarettes Really Aren't Cool

You would think that it would be difficult to sell items that are harmful to people. After all, you don't see people lining up to get beaten up or to have somebody cut off their toes. Pity then the poor cigarette manufacturer's task. Those companies sell a product that certifiably decreases life expectancy through its harmful role in lung cancers, strokes, and other major medical maladies. Yet millions of people around the world spend billions of dollars each year purchasing a product likely to send them to an early grave.

---

[118] Mark Leibovich, "For Paul Family, Libertarian Ethos Began at Home,' *The New York Times*, June 5, 2010.

No doubt what keeps cigarette smokers smoking are the addictive qualities of tobacco. Once hooked it requires nearly super human willpower to free oneself from the evil weed. A massive industry supports a tobacco free lifestyle, offering counseling, medicine, and placebos, and yet many people are unable to break their addiction.

The unintended consequence in this case arises from why people begin to smoke in the first place. Two reasons probably explain most first time smokers. The first is peer pressure; it is very hard to be the only kid in the car or on the street corner who isn't smoking. The second is image. Through product placement campaigns in movies and television, advertising in magazines, newspapers and at sporting events, and the ever present billboard along highways or on buses our society has been inculcated with the idea that "cool" people smoke. There was a time in movies that the hero always reached for a cigarette after vanquishing the villain or after a sexual encounter with a voluptuous costar. Consciously or subconsciously young people buy their first pack of cigarettes so that they can be cool too. The fact that a 14 year old first-time smoker tentatively puffing away on a cigarette looks decidedly uncool doesn't seem to register in the young person's mind. Somehow the media image of a superhero transcends the reality of a little kid looking foolish.

Looking foolish at 14 is not the unintended consequence of smoking. That occurs later in life as smoking takes its toll on the physical appearance and the mental acuity of smokers. If the subtle reason for smoking is to be cool then how ironic is it that as they age smokers show earlier signs of aging than do nonsmokers; their faces shrivel and show deeper wrinkles after smoking for as little as 10 years. And how cool is it to speak with an electronic voice after having one's vocal cords removed or how pretty is a face that is missing part of a jaw? When a smoker walks into the room you know it because their clothing and hair reek.

Culturally this odor was considered a manly smell a century ago but today amongst nonsmokers it is insufferable.

Worse still, when researchers reviewed data on over 23,000 smokers and nonsmokers they found that a one pack a day smoker had a 37% higher likelihood than a nonsmoker of having dementia; a smoker consuming 1 to 2 packs a day had a 44% higher risk; and those smoking more than two packs a day had twice the risk of dementia. [119] What an awful unintended consequence. Hoping to be cool, young people have consumed something which has made them super uncool. The unintended consequence of wanting to be cool by smoking cigarettes is that you are likely to look older when you'd really rather look younger, to suffer from lower endurance and physical ability, to possibly die at an earlier age, and even if you haven't died to wish that you had as your body falls into the snake pit of dementia and Alzheimer's disease.

Wherever you turn, smoking seems to be involved with unintended consequences. One aftermath of the subprime lending induced financial crisis was the decimation of many governmental budgets. In response, many states reduced their antismoking budgets thereby diminishing their successful public relations campaigns. [120] Nationwide, the Centers for Disease Control and Prevention reports that since states began an extensive anti-smoking campaign that the percentage of adult smokers has declined from approximately 25% in 1994 to slightly over 20% in 2009. The state of California which has one of the most directed

---

[119] Rachel A. Whitmer; William Thies, Samuel E. Gandy, Mount Sinai Professor of Alzheimer's Disease Research, Mount Sinai School of Medicine, New York City; Oct. 25, 2010, *Archives of Internal Medicine*, online.
[120] David Kesmogel and Betsy McKay, "Antismoking Programs are Slashed," *The Wall Street Journal*, November 9, 2010.

campaigns saw its adult smoking rate declined from nearly 23% in 1988 to just 13% in 2009. [121]

State budgets are in turmoil. Money is being foolishly saved, at least in the short term, as states reduce their spending on antismoking campaigns. It has been estimated that the annual cost to the US economy of smoking is nearly $200 billion which includes lost productivity and medical care[122]. The average state faces a $4 billion annual smoking bill. By contrast, the average state spends approximately $10 million a year fighting smoking. [123] An approximate return on investment from fighting smoking can be calculated using the numbers above. Without the 20% reduction in the number of smokers following the anti-smoking campaign, the average state would today face a $5 billion cost of smoking rather than a $4 billion cost. That is, annual expenditures of approximately $10 million have yielded approximately $1 billion in annual cost savings. The return on investment using these numbers is astronomical, in the thousands of percent a year.

The unintended consequence of states reducing their antismoking budgets is that their immediate savings, approximately $10 million a year, will be overwhelmed by higher smoking costs, possibly $1 billion annually if all former smokers return to the habit. The unintended consequence creates fiscal misadventure by the states. Rather than reducing antismoking spending states would have been more businesslike if they had raised it.

---

[121] Ibid.

[122] Hilary Smith, "The High Costs of Smoking," MSN Money. Retrieved September 10, 2008 from http://articles.moneycentral.msn.com.

[123] Op cit, Kesmogel and McKay, Source, Campaign for Tobacco Free Kids.

How Dams Create Damn Problems

Water is the essential elixir of life. Without it life as we know it cannot exist. The search for life in outer space always begins with the question is there any water? Arid earthbound locations invariably have limited plant and animal life. One strategy for holding onto water is to dam up rivers. Dam construction occurred as early as 3000 BC. [124] Modern dams create hydroelectricity, avert flooding and impound water for agricultural. People directly affected by improved access to water experience dramatic improvements in their lifestyles.

The unintended consequences of dams are varied and dramatic. By affecting a river's water flow a dam contributes to the loss of riverbeds and riverbanks. By blocking the natural movement of fish to breeding grounds a dam is likely to reduce spawning in the fish population. By changing the water table some scientists think that dams lead to dangerous seismic activity. By forcing communities to move out of the way of future water reservoirs lives are disrupted. By failing to control the force exerted by the water behind a dam, catastrophic disasters, such as the Buffalo Creek Flood, occur when dams break. It is uncertain how the calculus works out when comparing the benefits provided to populations using the power and water from a dam and costs from a dam's environmental damages. Not only is the final tally uncertain but those benefiting from the water see the problem through a different prism than do those harmed by its unintended consequences.

The Three Gorges Dam is a massive project begun in 1994 that spans the Yangtze River in the Hubei province of China. When the hydroelectric plant became fully operational in 2011 it produced as much electricity as 22

---

[124] S.W. Helms, "Jawa Excavations 1975, Third Preliminary Report," Levant, 1977

large nuclear or coal power stations. Electricity produced from hydroelectric stations averts the need to use fossil fuels. The Three Gorges Dam is China's one bright spot in in the environmental arena.

However, environmental problems caused by The Three Gorges Dam rival the scale of the dam itself. Its construction displaced over a million people with strong ancestral roots. Even the Chinese government has become concerned about environmental damages caused by the dam noting that "they may be triggering landslides, altering entire ecosystems and causing other serious environmental problems." [125] Others note that since the dam's construction there has been a substantial reduction in rainfall which has created serious drought conditions. The amount of forestation in the region has declined from approximately 20% in the 1950s to approximately 10% today. [126] Deforestation and the dam are accused by some of contributing to the 1998 flood of the Yangtze River. That flood killed more than 4,000 people, left more than 13 million homeless, and affected 240 million people.

The willingness of the Chinese government to face environmentalist's outrage as they propose extraordinary plans to alter the earth never seems to abate. The Chinese government has recently proposed to pump seawater thousands of miles to Xinjiang, an autonomous region wedged between Mongolia and India. [127] The water would be desalinated and used like fresh water with the bulk of it used to refill dried up salt lakes. Though it's still early days the project may get off the ground. More importantly, there

---

[125] Mara Hvistendahl, "China's Three Gorges Dam: An Environmental Catastrophe?" *Scientific American*, March 25, 2008.
[126] Qing, Dai, *The River Dragon Has Come!: The Three Gorges Dam and the Fate of China's Yangtze River and Its People* (East Gate Book), Armonk, New York: M.E. Sharpe, 1997.
[127] Jeremy Page, "China's Plan to Pump Seawater to Desert Divides Opinions," *The Wall Street Journal*, November 10, 2010.

seems to be almost no attention being given in the planning to the unintended consequences that such a project would engender.

How We Get Pissed When Things Come Back to Bite Us

The Chinese economic renaissance was arguably created in part by a systematic disregard for copyright laws and trademark protection. For years non-Chinese companies have complained fruitlessly about the country's disregard for their perceived rights. While it is true that different cultures have their own views on these two legal constructs, the Chinese have demonstrated little respect for Western efforts to treat intellectual property and brands, among other things, as intangible corporate assets protected against misuse and exploitation. Chinese knockoffs of DVDs/CDs, soft goods, pharmaceuticals, software and virtually everything which can be built are available for sale throughout the world at a vastly lower price then companies charge for original products. The losers from these transactions are recognizable and include artists, corporations, and defrauded consumers who mistakenly purchased a knockoff thinking it was real. The winners include Chinese companies which have richly profited and Chinese workers who have been employed by the counterfeit enterprises.

Recently tables have turned in an unintended consequence emanating from this environment condoning unbridled copyright infringement. DaVinci Furniture, a Chinese store with multiple outlets, has been accused in the Chinese media of selling knockoff Versace, Capelletti and Fendi items for full price as if they were genuine. [128] DaVinci's customers often spend hundreds of thousands of

---

[128] David Barboza, 2011, "Chinese Consumers Upset Over Counterfeit Furniture," *The New York Times*, July 19.

dollars decorating their homes with what they believe to be authentic imported luxury goods. The ruse apparently worked by Chinese factories shipping goods labeled as Italian imports to warehouses in Shanghai which were legally labeled as imports on the following day. [129]

The unintended consequence of tolerating (if not condoning) the methodical theft of intellectual property expropriated from foreign suppliers and artists is the creation of a culture in which such behavior is acceptable even when the victim is a neighbor. The reaction by Chinese consumers to the discovery of the apparent fraud has been strident and unrelenting. Ironically some of the individuals feeling aggrieved owe their newfound wealth to such unorthodox business practices themselves.

How to Compound Environmental Damage

When little or no thought is given to unintended consequences, well-meaning individuals may try to tackle environmental problems such as the uncontrolled growth of a species not natural to a locale by introducing another new species. Their thinking only goes as far as saying we don't want X and Y kills X therefore let's introduce Y. Little thought is given to how Y will be controlled. The US Department of Agriculture developed a strategy to reduce the number of salt cedar trees, a nonnative species in Colorado. [130] To combat this invading species the Department of Agriculture reached out to the country of Kazakhstan where it found a beetle that eats the leaves of the salt cedar tree. So in this equation, X was a tree and Y was a beetle.

---

[129] Ibid.

[130] Kirk Johnson, "In Battle of Bug vs. Shrub, Score One for the Bird," *The New York Times*, June 23, 2010.

The unintended consequence in the equation was the Southwestern Willow Flycatcher an endangered bird. Oddly, the bird seems to prefer to nest in salt cedar trees. [131] In other words, the Kazakhstan beetle was killing the very species that was saving an endangered bird. The equation now contains three variables, X, Y and Z. Z is the Southwestern Willow Flycatcher. By using Y to kill X the Department of Agriculture has caused an unintended consequence: the death of Z. The Department of Agriculture has now suspended the release of these beetles.

How Government Assistance Reduces Savings

In 1935, the Federal government passed the Social Security Act, the largest part of which is the Old-Age, Survivors, and Disability Insurance program. (Clearly this unintended consequence could easily have been presented in the chapter on governmental unintended consequences.) Social Security is the largest government program in the world spending $678 billion in 2010, an amount that excludes the $453 billion spent on Medicare and the $290 billion spent on Medicaid. While some argue for the privatization of these programs and while President Obama's National Commission on Fiscal Responsibility and Reform headed by Erskine Bowles a Democrat and Alan Simpson a Republican argue for raising the retirement age and payroll taxes, this book steps over those controversies to focus on unintended consequences caused by the Social Security program.

The Social Security program was enacted during the depression of the 1930s. At that time, a majority of the elderly lived in poverty. The first monthly Social Security payment was issued on January 31, 1940 in the amount of

---

[131] Ibid.

$22.54. [132] By 2010, the monthly payment had risen to $1,609 though the amount can vary depending upon a person's age when they retire and their average annual income prior to retirement (the smallest monthly payment is $199 and the largest is $2,929). While recipients of these checks cannot live in luxury, especially those without additional savings or pensions, for the most part they are able to live in comfortable dwellings and eat nourishing food.

Knowing that Social Security awaits them, workers have adjusted their savings rate downward. Data on personal savings rates are calculated by the Bureau of Economic Analysis. Unfortunately, that data begins in 1959 nearly two decades after the start of Social Security. In that year Americans saved 8.3% of their disposable income after the payment of taxes. My personal guess is that the personal savings rate was higher during the war years, the early 1940s, and possibly higher as well during the depression, 1929 - 1939. Americans continued to save about 8% of their disposable income throughout most of the 1960s, then the savings rate increased in the 1970s rising to as high as 15%, and then started to fall (excepting during recessionary periods when it rose back up) until it was less than 1% in the middle 2000s.

There are many explanations for why the savings rate declined from nearly 10% to less than 1%. For example, Americans acquired homes and the value of those homes increased which individuals may have considered to be a portion of their savings. Another argument is that people expecting a sizable Social Security check when they retire, lose the incentive to reduce current consumption in favor of future consumption. That is, their personal savings rate declines. The unintended consequence of the establishment of a Social Security program is that people stop saving for their retirement. Unfortunately some people will discover

---

[132] Research Note #3: Details of Ida May Fuller's Payroll Tax Contributions, Social Security Administration.

upon retirement that the size of their Social Security payment is insufficient to allow them to live their desired lifestyle.

Strangely good and bad things come from a lower savings rate. The good is that having a society of spenders (as opposed to savers) partially explains the dramatic growth in the American economy since the 1970s. Contrast the health of the American economy with that in Japan, a society of inveterate savers. The Japanese economy has been in the doldrums since 1990. The savings rate in Japan is higher because their social security system is less generous than in the US. The Japanese savings rate was in the range of 20% of income throughout the 1970s and 1980s. Since then the rate has fallen to about 2%.

Social Security or some similar system to protect widows and orphans and individuals unable to work due to physical or mental handicaps is a necessity in a modern society. Extending that to include healthy working individuals who have the capacity to save for their own retirement creates an unintended consequence that pushes savings in the society downward. Without savings it is difficult for an economy to invest. Lacking adequate savings the US has borrowed money from abroad giving our creditor nations such as China, Japan, and countries in Europe more political power in Washington.

How Total Savings React to Forced Savings

There are some things that everybody knows are good for them: exercise, eating right, and saving for retirement amongst others. The problem is how to get people to act on this knowledge. The two basic strategies involve the carrot or the stick. With the stick as the motivator, people not doing enough exercise might lose their job, who don't eat right might not be allowed to live in certain neighborhoods, or who don't save might not be allowed to buy beer or wine. When the carrot is used to change behavior, people are motivated to do something by offering them something desirable; an attractive new town swimming pool might result in an increase in the number of people swimming, serving free helpings of healthy food might result in people ordering fewer hamburgers or pizzas, and creating programs to allow people to save money without actively doing anything might increase the number of savers and the amount that they save.

In 2006, Congress passed the Pension Protection Act. A provision of the Act allows companies to automatically enroll employees in 401(k) plans. In cases where the employer has chosen automatic enrollment, employees must now opt out of participation in the plan otherwise they are participants. This program, designed to increase the number of employees participating in 401(k) plans, is a carrot incentive plan. It makes it very easy for employees to save for retirement.

The *Wall Street Journal* uncovered an unintended consequence of the Pension Protection Act.[133] While it was true that more companies opted to automatically enroll employees in 401(k) plans, thereby resulting in more savers, the amount that these employees saved, on average, was significantly lower than the amount they would have saved had they voluntarily enrolled in the plan. That is, active savings decisions made prior to the Pension Protection Act generally resulted in a higher savings rate (5% to 10% of income) than the amount saved when the employer was permitted to set the contribution rate (generally at 3%).

Employees who have been voluntarily enrolled in a 401(k) plan are permitted to increase their savings rate above the amount their employer sets; that is, they could save 5 or 10% if they wished. The *Wall Street Journal* analysis discovered that people experience an ennui affect about how much to save when someone else makes the initial decision

---

[133] Anne Tergesen, "401(k) Law Suppresses Saving for Retirement," *The Wall Street Journal*, July 7, 2011.

for them about their participation in the plan. This unintended consequence is similar to the experience of individuals living under a dictatorship. Knowing that the dictator makes most decisions causes individuals to make none. That causality helps explain the lack of entrepreneurship in countries ruled by dictators.

A second unintended consequence, and actually a humorous one, arises in this case of 401(k) plans. The *Wall Street Journal* team discovered that most companies opted for a 3% contribution rate for their 401(k) plans because an IRS document describing its regulations used that figure as its example. Despite the IRS' noting that the 3% figure was only an example and not a mandate, the fear of lawsuits led to the unintended consequence that whatever the government writes down or says, in this case a 3% savings rate is what companies did. Like frightened lambs, we sometimes seek safety when none is required.

How Human Ignorance Creates Hatred

Probably the greatest scourge to harm the human race is the Black Death – also known as the Black Plague, the bubonic plague and scientifically as the bacterium Yersinia Pestis. In its first known visitation in the sixth century, the Justinian plague, Yersinia Pestis wiped out 50% of Europe's population. [134] After the year 750 the plague seemed to vanish and it did not resurface in Europe again until the 14th century when it was thought to have reduced the world's population from approximately 450 million people to 350 million.[135] In this it's second pass over the earth, now called the Black Plague, the bacteria killed at least 100 million people. Sporadic but deadly reoccurrences of the plague

---

[134] "Plague, Plague Information, Black Death Facts News, Photos– National Geographic". Science.nationalgeographic.com.
[135] J. N. Hays, 2005, *Epidemics and Pandemics; their Impacts on Human History*, ABC-CLIO, page 23.

continued until the middle 1800s. The final great surfacing of Yersinia Pestis began in 1894 in the Yunnan Province of China.[136] From there it spread throughout the world including an outbreak in 1899 in Hawaii and again in San Francisco in 1900. The death toll in India alone was 10 million people. [137]

Recently scientists have unequivocally confirmed that the cause of the plague was the bacteria Yersinia Pestis. Their effort included forensic analysis of grave sites dating back as far as 1347. [138] The bacteria's normal hosts are rodents such as rats or voles; infection of people occurs due to their proximity to rodent populations. The lack of cleanliness and adequate sanitation in large cities quickly spread the disease once it had jumped from rodents to people. Unfortunately this epidemiologic understanding occurred hundreds of years after the plague hit an ignorant and highly superstitious population.

At the time of the plagues, bacteria was unknown and the idea that a microscopic organism could spread disease would probably have been considered blasphemous. Medical practitioners could not account for the disease. People believed that the plague was a punishment from G-d for their impious behavior or was possibly a result of earthquakes. [139] But those explanations did not provide them with a means to strike back. Perversely humans believe that if I can blame someone else and hurt or kill them then I am doing something about my problem. Having somebody to blame seems to placate the human psyche. The Jewish population was not well integrated in mainstream society. Their religious customs and style of dress set them apart from their contemporaries. Most importantly, they engaged in money

---

[136] Nicholas Wade, "Black Deaths Origins Traced to China," *The New York Times*, November 1, 2010.
[137] "Infectious Diseases: Plague Through History, sciencemag.org.
[138] Wade, Op Cit.
[139] J. M. Bennett and C. W. Hollister, *Medieval Europe: A Short History* (New York: McGraw-Hill, 2006), p. 326.

lending activities since they were not conscribed from doing so by their religion, and as has been true in every financial crisis, bankers and lenders are blamed when creditors are unable to repay loans. Who better to blame for the Black Plague then a group which looks different, which worships differently, and whose demise would relieve some of their financial burden?

An unintended consequence of the Black Plague was how it created and spread a virulent form of anti-Semitism. This religious hatred attained semi-official institutional blessing throughout Europe (Emperor Charles IV of Bohemia and Peter IV of Aragon tried to protect their Jews). [140] Jewish communities suffered from the plague alongside their non-Jewish counterparts though possibly to a lesser extent because Jewish laws require dead bodies to be buried within a day. At first Jews were accused of poisoning the water wells of Christians. Throughout Europe, except in Avignon where the Pope protected them, Jews were burned and their communities were sacked. [141] Foreshadowing the atrocities committed by the Third Reich during the 1940s, 210 Jewish communities throughout Europe were obliterated. [142] Many of the Jews left alive after the maelstrom had moved to Poland or Lithuania though some remained in Central Europe. [143]

This unintended consequence, perhaps more than others, had a permanent impact. Hatred unlike love is an emotion that grows over time compounding itself when the feelings are reinforced by fellow travelers. The history of anti-Semitism traces back to ancient times beginning with

---

[140] Ami Isseroff, March 31, 2009, discusses anti Semitism in http://www.zionism-israel.com/dic/Black_Death_Jews.htm.
[141] Jacob Marcus, *The Jew in the Medieval World: A Sourcebook, 315-1791*, (New York: JPS, 1938), 43-48
[142] http://www.jewishhistory.org.il/history.php?startyear=1340&endyear=1349
[143] Ami Isseroff, Op Cit.

antipathy towards the religion by Greek and Roman writers, becoming restrictions against Jewish customs, and growing into pogroms of indiscriminate killing as early as 38 A.D. [144] In modern times, the irrational feelings of hatred toward this "other group", people practicing the Jewish religion, has seemed to grow and expand as one group of anti-Semites assumes the mantle of hatred after a previous group's hatred has abated or been controlled. Muslim pogroms in the early 11th century were satisfied with forced conversions but when the mantle of hatred passed to the crusaders later in the 11th century, massacres occurred. Killings during the Black Plague were no doubt easier to condone following the spillage of Jewish blood by the crusaders. In more recent times, intolerant practices (and occasional pogroms) in Prussia, Bohemia, and Russia culminated in the mass killings of Jews during the Holocaust in Nazi Germany.

As one further step in the progression of anti-Semitism, the Black Plague's unintended consequence, blaming Jews for a bacterial infection, perpetuated a blemish on the face of humanity. How different the world might be today if anti-Semitism's many victims had survived.

How Human Ignorance Creates Hatred: Part 2

In 2006 Niall Ferguson wrote *The War of the World* a colossal study of the 20th century. [145] He argues that the 20th century has been the most violent in modern history despite the fact that astonishing scientific and intellectual advances were concurrently made. Ferguson argues that the source of most of these wars, genocides, and atrocities is

---

[144] Anti-Semitism, *Wikipedia*, November 15, 2010.
[145] Niall Ferguson, 2006, *The War of the World: 20th century Conflict and the Descent of the West,* The Penguin Press.

"ethnic conflict, [from] economic volatility in the decline of empires." [146]

Ethnic violence/hatred is not new to the 20th century. Earlier examples include pogroms in Eastern Europe, the American Ku Klux Klan, and the destruction of Indian cultures in North America. What is new to the 20th century is the belief, perhaps fostered by its success in America, that ethnic groups can be intermingled within small geographic areas and live in harmony. Ferguson disagrees. He argues that ethnic violence begins when groups are mixed and not before. If he is right, then the unintended consequence of attempts to encourage different ethnic groups to comingle may be ethnic conflict.

An example of the unintended consequence of mixing races has recently occurred in Karachi Pakistan. Karachi has long been populated by a majority of ethnic Mohajirs. [147] In recent times 5 million Pashtuns have moved into Karachi, not because of a governmental social program, but to avoid the war zone on the Pakistani/Afghanistan border. Behaving like any dominant group would when it perceived a threat from an immigrating minority, the two sides, Mohajirs and Pashtuns have fought a bloody internecine battle. Nearly 3,000 people were murdered in Karachi by the two groups in 2010 - perhaps not a large figure for a city of 18 million but a huge tragedy for affected families.

The idealized world depicted in advertisements of multiple ethnic groups reclining peacefully below cumulus clouds while wild beast wander tranquilly amongst them is probably unachievable in the world as we know it. Efforts to

---

[146] Simon Sebag Montefiore, "Century of Rubble," *The New York Times Sunday Book Review*, November 12, 2006.

[147] Jane Perlez, "Karachi Turns Deadly, Diverted by Bitter Rivalries in Pakistan," *The New York Times*, August 19, 2010.

supplant this natural law are likely to encounter the same unintended consequence as has bedeviled Pakistan.

How Taking Care of the Future Helps the Present

Not all unintended consequences turn out bad. Sometimes people do things and then receive a positive extra benefit as a result of an unintended consequence. One example occurred in a town called Ixtlan de Juarez in Mexico. The Zapotec Indians who inhabit the town in a Southern Mexican State had battled to obtain the right to manage the 48,000 acres of forests in their state. [148] Once they attained this authority, their opposition to a get rich quick mentality, lead the Zapotec to conserve their forest rather than to cut them down.

Forestry like wine making is an unhurried business. Trees take decades to mature and until they do the forester sees only costs and no revenue. Less thoughtful foresters might clear-cut a property without planting any new seedlings. With that business model, costs are minimized and the revenue stream is hurried up. The Zapotec mindful of the alternatives chose the slow process. Knowing that it would take time for the forest to prove economic they developed a lumber business.

The unintended consequence of the decision to conserve and manage their 48,000 acre forest is that the Zapotec now have a lumber business that employs 300 people. Harvested wood is no longer simply cut down and exported but is now fashioned into furniture by local residents. [149] The Zapotec's positive unintended

---

[148] Elisabeth Malkin, "Growing a Forest and Harvesting Jobs," *The New York Times*, November 23, 2010.
[149] Ibid.

consequence is that they have created a future for their children.

How Protecting Liberty Leads to Foolish Behavior

Civil liberties are fundamental to the American way of life. These rights span the very basic, such as the right to life, to the more complex such as the freedom of assembly. One such liberty is freedom from persecution because of who one is; this includes one's religion, gender, or national origin.

The obligation to protect Americans against terrorism runs counter to the desire to maintain civil liberties. The threat of terrorism has changed how we live. For example, when traveling by air our luggage cannot be locked to protect our possessions from other's eyes and sticky fingers and it is now subject to thorough searches. Where we once could arrive at airports with minutes to spare we must now arrive 90 minutes early in order to go through security. The Transportation Safety Administration (TSA) has introduced full body x-ray scanners, that some argue is intrusive. Passengers opting out of the potentially dangerous radiation exposure from full-body x-ray scanners are then subjected to searches that are so thorough that civil libertarians would have protested strongly just a few years ago.

The unintended consequence of our faith that civil liberties are of the utmost importance is that we treat all people alike and view everyone as a potential terrorist rather than focusing search efforts on likely terrorist candidates. Someone in their 80s or 90s, who looks like your grandmother or grandfather, is as likely to be thoroughly searched by the TSA as are other candidates who appear to be more dangerous. Americans choose candidates for searches randomly rather than scientifically. It is certainly true that a 90-year-old person can carry a bomb; however, the probability of that being true is low. In contrast, the probability that a young person possibly of Middle Eastern descent and possibly unable to speak English is carrying a bomb is far greater. And yet America persists in putting civil liberties before everything else and force, for example, elderly passengers to be subjected to unwanted and intrusive body searches.

Countries even more concerned about the threat of terrorism then the US such as Israel approach the problem of passenger screening through a different lens. For them, civil liberties take a backseat to the ultimate need for identifying and arresting terrorist. The Israeli methods use early detection techniques. [150] Once the Israelis think that a passenger is a potential terrorist they subject that individual to screening efforts even more invasive than those now used in the US. One technique relies on intensive one-on-one questioning of suspects to catch them in a lie. [151]

How Giving Help without Getting Something in Exchange Breeds Problems

Human behavior is remarkable and funny at the same time. An example of its remarkableness is how people pick themselves up after adversity and get on with their lives. Stories abound of Holocaust survivors, people living with serious illness, and those who have lost loved ones who go on to live generous and productive lives. An example of a funny aspect of human behavior surfaces in connection with altruism.

---

[150] Helene Cooper, "Some Suggest US Look at Israeli Airport Screening Methods," *The New York Times*, November 23, 2010.
[151] Ibid.

There is a long history of the fortunate providing help to the needy. Generosity appears across the political spectrum and involves every religious belief. Historically, the Roman Emperor Trajan provided assistance to the poor. In the 17th century the English Poor Laws gave the responsibility for helping those in need to local parishes. [152] In the US, the first national welfare effort was the Emergency Relief Act of 1932 which had a $300 million appropriation. Despite these efforts poverty has never been vanquished.

There are many ways in which needy people can be helped ranging from outright gifts, in cash or in-kind, to exchanges which demand something in return for the assistance. Both approaches are used in the US. For example, food stamps officially known as the United States Supplemental Nutrition Assistance Program (SNAP) provides assistance to 40 million Americans. The average benefit of a recipient was $133.12 in June 2009. [153] Nothing is expected from recipients in exchange for these benefits. Recipients are given a card which is used at the supermarket to purchase food. [154] In contrast, after the passage under President Clinton of the Personal Responsibility and Work Opportunity Reconciliation Act of 1996 the federal government "ended welfare as we know it." [155] The bill ended welfare as an entitlement by requiring recipients to work after receiving benefits for a period of two years and limiting benefits to a period of five years.

Every society has an element which is unable to provide for itself financially. Whether as a result of illness, accident, lack of education, birth related problems, or short-

---

[152] EH.Net, *The Poor Laws of England*, Economic History Association.

[153] Roberta Rampton, "Food Stamp List Soars Past 35 million: USDA". *Reuters*, September 3, 2009.

[154] Agribusiness has an obvious interest in this form of relief.

[155] Bill Clinton, October 23, 1991, "The New Covenant: Responsibility and Rebuilding the American Community. Remarks to Students at Georgetown University," *Democratic Leadership Council*.

term economic fluctuations there will always be those who are unable to fully take care of themselves. A society that ignores extreme cases of need gives rise to the most severe forms of deprivation. Art and literature have always used these situations as a canvas to depict mankind at its worst; vivid depictions of poverty scorch the minds of even the hardest hearted individual.

Whether it is a result of seeing the effects of poverty or generosity naturally occurs, modern society has attempted to alleviate a portion of this misery. More generous nations such as Norway provide health benefits, living accommodations, furniture and food to the less fortunate; as a consequence, fewer than 2% of Norwegians live in poverty as compared to about 12% in the US. [156] Less generous nations usually provide some form of food supplement to at least keep people from starving to death.

The US is neither the most or the least generous when it comes to assisting underprivileged residents. Individual Americans are extremely generous and can always be relied on to send assistance when disaster strikes anywhere in the world. Their legislators mirror this generosity at home with programs that include food stamps, welfare benefits, public housing, and health benefits. That is where the unintended consequence begins.

Fortunately, the US is a wealthy nation. As such it is able to provide relatively generous benefits to the less fortunate among its citizens. That is how it is, how it should be, and how the voters want it. Of course, voters and legislators are not required to consider the unintended consequences of their actions. In 1983, according to the US Census Bureau, 29.6% of US households received governmental benefits. The portion of Americans receiving governmental benefits rises nearly monotonically after that until 2008.

Government benefits are designed to relieve poverty and improve the lives of the needy. Living in a rich country

---

[156] L., Kenworthy, 1999, "Do Social-Welfare Policies Reduce Poverty? A Cross-National Assessment," *Social Forces, 77*(3), 1119-1139.

one would expect that the portion of the population receiving these benefits would not increase in fact it might even decline as the improved living standards allowed for the acquisition of skills and education. Why then has the portion of Americans receiving governmental benefits risen? The unintended consequence of generous benefits appears to be that more people find public assistance to be a reasonable alternative to work. Not only do 44.4% of Americans now receive governmental benefits but as of 2010 fully 45% of Americans paid no taxes to the federal government.[157] It would seem then that as a result of this unintended consequence we have approximately half of the population supporting the other half. More was said on this topic earlier in chapter 2, see How Pandering to Constituents Creates a Politically Unstable Situation.

Professor Walter Williams of George Mason University has spoken poignantly comparing his experience as a young African-American growing up in the 1940s to the situation of poor African-Americans today. He describes how 75% to 85% of black children lived in two-parent families in the 1940s.[158] The percentage today is probably in the single digits. Williams says that "the welfare state has done ...what slavery could not do, what Jim Crow couldn't do, what the harshest racism couldn't do... and that is destroy the black family."[159] What began as a program to help the poor and indigent has instead irreparably harmed an entire community of Americans because of an unintended consequence.

Human behavior responds to signals. Generosity seems to affect the desire to work. Recently, the Obama administration lengthened to 99 weeks the period of time during which people can receive unemployment

[157] Sara Murray, "Obstacle to Deficit Cutting: A Nation of Entitlements, *The Wall Street Journal*, September 15, 2010

[158] Jason L Riley, "The State Against Blacks - The Weekend Interview with Walter Williams," *The Wall Street Journal*, January 22-23, 2011.

[159] Ibid.

compensation. [160] There is anecdotal evidence that some people have stopped looking for work or have turned down jobs because they find their unemployment payments to be sufficient. The amount of money provided by unemployment insurance compensation varies across states. The state with the highest payments is Massachusetts, a maximum payment of $942 a week with a minimum of $628. In contrast, Mississippi provides $230 a week. [161] With a national minimum wage of $7.25 an hour and a 40 hour workweek generating $290 a week in pay, money collected from unemployment plus food stamps may be too attractive. The average rank and file worker earned $780.33 a week in November 2010 according to the Bureau of Labor Statistics. In many cases $780 a week is not that much above the level of unemployment compensation (including food stamp payments). Too much generosity can destroy the economic rationale for working. That is, it makes sense for some people to continue to receive unemployment compensation rather than to accept a new job at a wage that is lower than desired.[162] This unintended consequence may explain the long duration of high unemployment rates long after the end of the recession, in June 2009.

A counter argument notes how the distribution of income has recently skewed to favor the wealthy. Advocates suggest that wage levels are too low at the tail of the income distribution. The higher compensation paid to skilled workers lends some support to this distributional argument

---

[160] States provide 26 weeks of coverage. The federal government extends coverage beyond this period. The Obama administration enacted several federal programs that extended unemployment benefits for up to an additional 73 weeks beyond the state chartered 26 weeks.

[161] Website, File Unemployment, December 3, 2010.

[162] The average length of unemployment in November 2010 was approximately 34 weeks suggesting that not all people view the taking of unemployment compensation payments as either a right or as an alternative to work.

but a willingness to live on less many also explain a portion of the inequality.

What about compassionate giving when it comes to healthcare? Isn't the moral thing to require hospitals and doctors to care for patients who come for treatment regardless of their ability to pay for the treatment? When I polled my students there was near unanimous assent to this proposition. But then I asked the question who would pay the bills? Their response was society would. But what if society has run out of money? That question is becoming true for states, the federal government, and other nations. In October 2010, the State of Arizona ended payments for certain transplant operations among the uninsured.[163] That is, Arizona began to treat insured and uninsured individuals differently. Some would say immorally.

How insurance companies make decisions about what procedures to pay for is somewhat mysterious. In Arizona prior to the legislators approving the restrictions on transplants, the state's Medicaid agency gathered data for analysis. It found that 13 of 14 patients who received nonrelated bone marrow transplants died within six months. [164] These procedures each cost the state as much as several hundred thousand dollars. While no one can say how much six months of life is worth, it is sometimes the case that the coffers run dry. That is what appears to have happened in Arizona. There is only so much that can be given no matter how great the need.

The practice of medical tourism by indigent patients is another unintended consequence that arises from the generosity of wealthy nations. Medical tourism occurs when someone travels to another country for medical treatment. When it involves someone traveling to a wealthy country to

---

[163] Marc Lacey, "Transplant Patients Put at Risk by a State's Financial Distress," *The New York Times*, December 3, 2010.
[164] Ibid.

obtain free medical care that they could not afford and would not have obtained in their home country, medical tourism becomes an unintended consequence of the generosity of wealthy nations. American hospitals and physicians follow the Hippocratic Oath which in part says "I will remember that I remain a member of society, with special obligations to all my fellow human beings, though sound of mind and body as well as the infirm." When a sick person arrives at the emergency room they are not denied medical care regardless of their citizenship status. A number of cases have been published in the press describing multimillion dollar cost to hospitals to provide extreme medical care to noncitizens some of whom have come directly from the airport to the hospital. [165]

Combining a generous health-care system with the 14th Amendment passed in 1868 which provides citizenship to anyone born in the US, referred to as birthright citizenship, gives rise to another unintended consequence that also involves hospital care. Women around the world, often among the wealthiest in their own societies, are traveling to the US to have their babies. [166] The complicated issues of citizenship, future familial immigration, and Social Security and long-term care notwithstanding, these births impose a financial hardship on American hospitals. With an average delivery cost at an American hospital approaching $30,000 per baby, the aggregate cost of medical tourists grows burdensome. This unintended consequence is about more than just medical tourism, but the initial cost impact falls on those parties paying medical bills.

---

[165] Dana Canedy, "Hospitals Feeling Strained from Illegal Immigrants," *The New York Times*, August 25, 2002; Chris L Jenkins, "Benefits for Illegal Immigrants Targeted," *Washington Post*, February 9, 2005; and Paul Harasim, "Concerns Rise Over Uninsured," *Las Vegas Review-Journal*, August 18, 2009.
[166] Jennifer Medina, "Arriving as Pregnant Tourist, Leaving with American Babies," *The* New York Times, March 28, 2011.

Giving charity and sharing with others are a beautiful human trait. Human behavior is like water leaking through a roof; it follows the path of least resistance. When people are given something for nothing they come to expect it and they demand more of it. Every society needs to calibrate what it is willing to take from one group and give to another. Otherwise they will face extraordinary demands as an unintended consequence of their compassion.

How Grade Inflation Drives Out Good Teachers and Other Problems

An ongoing debate concerns academic grades and whether they have needlessly risen. Notwithstanding the question of whether the increase in grades are justified or not, higher grades have produced an important unintended consequences. If an A grade means exceptional work, a B grade means very good work and a C grade means average or what is expected then it is hard to imagine all students in a class receiving A grades. Yet some schools report an average grade of A in sections of 200 students. [167] Some notable institutions have taken a stand against grade inflation. Princeton University for example has a guideline restricting A grades to no more than 35% of a class; the graduate school of business at Northeastern University limits A's and A-'s to 50% or fewer of registered students (employers don't pay for classes receiving a grade less than a B).

This book is not the appropriate place to debate the topic of grade inflation. It is however the correct forum to discuss the many unintended consequences arising from grade inflation. To begin consider the purpose served by assigning grades. In a simplistic view, grades perform a triage function: separating out the best students from the

---

[167] Tamara Lewin, "A Quest to Explain What Grades Really Mean," *The New York Times*, December 25, 2010.

worst with everybody else in the middle. While some students might prefer that all enrollees receive the highest grade, potential employers need to know more about the student then that they merely attended the class. When grade inflation takes place, the unintended consequence is that employers use other mechanisms to make hiring decisions - college attended, race, attractiveness, height, and other less critical measures. The alternative selection methods help Ivy League students, those of the same race as the employer, the more attractive and the tallest. A student who works hard and acquires mastery of the new topic is shortchanged by grade inflation. Their achievements fail to stand out. One unintended consequence of grade inflation is that hard work does not get rewarded.

When a college has two classes one of which teaches an important topic with grades assigned in that class based on merit and a second class which teaches nothing of value but in which all students get the top grade, virtually all students will choose to take the worthless class in order to defend their grade point average (GPA). [168] Students are known to make use of online resources which report on the grading difficulty of various instructors when selecting classes to take. The second unintended consequence of grade inflation is that the education being given to students and dearly paid for by parents has been dumbed down.

Students select which college to attend based on a number of factors including the college's ability to help their long-run career. If students believe that their GPA will influence their ability to get the job or career they seek, then they may choose colleges based on comparative information about average GPAs. The unintended consequence of that approach to college selection would be to distribute students disproportionately to institutions awarding the highest grades and not to those providing the most opportunity or knowledge. This unintended consequence may even have

---

[168] Ibid.

macro effects if it explains why US students score lower than students in other countries on achievement tests. It may partly explain why we have fallen behind some of our trading partners. In mathematics the US scores beneath 30 countries; while in the sciences there are 22 countries scoring ahead of the US. [169] If Americans were more concerned with knowledge and less concerned with GPAs these deficits might be smaller.

A final unintended consequence related to grade inflation has less to do with course content and more to do with the grading procedure. Students probably prefer classes that not only give high grades but which evaluate their performance with non-test mechanisms such as paper writing, field-trip exercises, or team presentations. While non-test assessment instruments provide excellent data of student performance, it is hard to top a well-prepared examination for ferreting out what students have learned. Also, by avoiding examinations students encounter another unintended consequence which is the fact that taking a test actually helps them to learn. [170] Students who took a test about what they had read had 50% greater recall a week later than did students who just read the same piece without the examination. [171]

How Some Knowledge Can be too Much Knowledge

Practically everyone knows that radiation is dangerous. The term radioactivity was coined by the Nobel

---

[169] Lauren Etter, "American Teens Trail Global Peers in Math Scores," *The Wall Street Journal*, December 7, 2010.

[170] Pam Belluck, "Take a Test to Really Learn, Research Suggests," *The New York Times*, January 21, 2011.

[171] Jeffrey D. Karpicke and Janell R Blunt, "Retrieval Practice Produces More Learning than Elaborative Studying with Concept Mapping," *Science*, January 20, 2011.

prize-winning scientist Marie Curie. Unfortunately she died of aplastic anemia as a result of exposure to radiation. Radiation's dangers are better known today. Nonetheless, the media barrages people with information on alleged health hazards without providing supporting scientific evidence. As a result, an unintended consequence occurs when a partially informed individual overreacts to incomplete information.

An example is full body scanners which are used at airports for security purposes. A number of individuals (ignoring those with civil liberties concerns) overreacted to the news that airports would begin using full body scanners and objected to them forcing the TSA to institute a policy wherein pat downs could be used instead. *The New York Times* article, "Radiation in the Dentist's Chair," compares the amount of radiation a person absorbs in a full body scan and from other devices. [172] A chest x-ray has 100 times greater absorption of radiation than a body scan; a CT head scan has nearly 2,100 times more absorption of radiation than a full body airports scan. Though most people don't realize that radiation is absorbed during air travel itself, it is worth noting that during a cross-country flight from New York City to Los Angeles a person absorbs 50 times more radiation from the flight then from the preflight airport body scan.

Similar unsubstantiated fears have led families to not vaccinate their children against common childhood illnesses such as measles or meningitis. As Dr. Mark Sawyer a pediatrician and infectious disease specialist in San Diego said, "Most of these parents have never seen measles, and don't realize it could be a bad disease so they turn their concerns to unfounded risks. They do not perceive risk of the disease but perceive risk of the vaccine." [173] Having a little

---

[172] Walt Bogdanich and Joe Craven McGinty, "Radiation in the Dentist Chair," *The New York Times*, November 22, 2010.
[173] Jennifer Steinhauer, "Public Health Risk Seen as Parents Reject Vaccines," *The New York Times*, March 21, 2008.

knowledge creates the unintended consequence of thinking we know something when in fact we really don't.

How Some Knowledge Can be too Much Knowledge: Part 2

Germs are everywhere. But all germs are not bad for humans. See the section, How Strength Leads to Weakness, in Chapter 4. Knowing that some germs are harmful has led people to alter their behavior in strange ways. Knowing that germs are everywhere has led some individuals to overuse antibacterial agents on their bodies (with antibacterial soaps) and in their homes (with antibacterial solutions). This overuse of antiseptics such as isopropyl alcohol, hydrogen peroxide, and iodine has resulted in the unintended consequence that some bacteria have evolved to become immune to the effects of these agents. Not being able to combat bacteria when it is needed, such as during surgery, can be life-threatening.

A second unintended consequence that arises because people know a little something about germs is how individuals think they can protect themselves from germs while in a public bathroom. At the urinals in the men's room the bowl is frequently left unflushed by men fearful of touching the handle (science has come to the rescue with the invention of the automatic flushing toilet). Other men take a piece of paper towel that they've used to dry their hands, use it to open the bathroom door, and then drop it on the floor creating an unsanitary mess. Some public bathrooms have moved the receptacle for used towels near to the door to avoid this problem but design limitations limit this solution.

A third unintended consequence is that some people do not touch things as they interact with stores, stairs and other people. While there is nothing wrong per se with not touching displays in stores, holding onto railings on stairs, or shaking hands with other people, the strategy fails if for example a person falls down the stairs

How Sports Can be Bad for Your Health

Working out is good for your health. Lack of exercise is partially responsible for the obesity epidemic in America. Becoming more active whether it is walking, running, rowing, etc. can improve cardiovascular health, impact diabetes, and improve mental health. As long as exercise/sports are done in moderation they are helpful. Overdoing sports can lead to unintended consequences.

Tennis elbow, golfer's shoulder, runner's knee are all examples of common injuries afflicting athletes who overdo their workouts especially when they limit them to the same activity. Doing two or three different exercises is less likely to produce an overuse injury. Professional athletes do not have the luxury of playing tennis one day and golf the next; their overuse injuries are inescapable. In contrast, amateur athletes can escape the unintended consequence from overdoing one sport by instituting a rigorous exercise management program.

Overuse injuries are especially critical to avoid with adolescent athletes since their "careers" are brief. Common overuse injuries amongst younger athletes include Osgood-Slater disease which afflicts their knees, Sever's disease which afflicts their heel growth plate and elbow and shoulder injuries amongst baseball players. [174] Avoiding this unintended consequence should be a high priority for juvenile coaches.

---

[174] Jane E Brody, "A Warning on Overuse Injuries for Youths," *The New York Times*, April 5, 2011.

How Say's Law Still Applies

The expression 'supply creates its own demand' is attributed to John Maynard Keynes and is thought to be his caricature of Say's Law. [175] A similar idea is heard in the phrase "if you build it, he will come" from the movie *Field of Dreams*. The thought is that people are attracted to whatever is available.

When it comes to resource allocation the expression supply creates its own demand is an unintended consequence. For example, the naïve remedy for urban traffic congestion is to build more roads. The remedy doesn't alleviate clogged highways because as several economists have discovered new road construction has the unintended consequence of creating new traffic. [176] They found that within 10 years of building more highways that the proportionate increase in highway miles was matched exactly by a proportionate increase in vehicle miles driven.

The same unintended consequence is bedeviling the new middle class in China. Automobiles are among the first purchases made by the newly wealthy Chinese middle-class. Cars are for transportation and to communicate their newfound wealth. [177] The problem is that so many people have bought cars, 2,000 a day in Beijing alone, that there is virtually nowhere to drive without endlessly sitting in traffic. Sales of cars in China in 2010 are 35% higher than in 2009 which themselves were 46% higher than in 2008.[178] Traffic congestion in China will probably be attacked in a manner

---

[175] Say's Law actual describes the factors required for there to be an excess supply of a product.

[176] Gilles Duranton and Matthew A Turner, "The Fundamental Law of Road Congestion: Evidence From US Cities," *American Economic Review,* Vol 101, No. 6, 2012.

[177] Michael Wines, "Cars Multiply, But the Chinese Still Can't Find a Fast Lane," *The New York Times*, December 27, 2010.

[178] Ibid.

similar to the way Mao got rid of the four pests (see How Biologist Must Not Have Been on Noah's Ark in Chapter 5) or how China built the world's largest dam complex (see above, How Dams Create Damn Problems) - with brute force and too little planning. In other words, it is likely that further unintended consequences will arise as more Chinese consumers buy automobiles, road congestion increases, and as poorly designed solutions are implemented.

How Birthdays Relate to Death

The day a person dies, all other things equal, should fall with equal probability across the calendar. There should be no greater likelihood of a person dying for example just before or just after their birthday. It appears that an unintended consequence of being famous is that people somehow have the power to forestall death until just after their birthday.[179] Perhaps the most intriguing example of death postponement by famous people, even though it was not their own birthday but the birthday of our country, were the deaths of John Adams and Thomas Jefferson, two of the most famous signers of the Declaration of Independence. They both died on the same day in 1826 -the 4TH of July. Their deaths occurred precisely 50 years after the Declaration of Independence was signed. John Adams' last words were purportedly "Thomas Jefferson survives."

The scientific literature does not fully support the postponed death hypothesis for populations of normal, non-famous people. Some researchers report they have not been able to replicate David P Phillips's work for everyday people but others have indicated similar or related findings. For example, a study looking at nearly 3 million individuals found that women were more likely to die in the week after

---

[179] David P Phillips, as explained in G. Smith, *Statistical Reasoning*, 3RD edition New York: McGraw-Hill, 1991, pages 477-479.

their birthday than during any other week of the year.[180] Another study found that suicides by people over the age of 75 were disproportionately performed in the month following their birthday. [181] Other studies have shown a similar will to live having the ability to postpone death until after holidays, both the Jewish Passover and the Chinese New Year[182]. Other scientists have not found an association between birthdays and death[183]. As far as unintended consequences go, this one appears to be beneficial. It enables people within sight of their birthday or an important holiday to live a little longer.

[180] David P Phillips, CA Van Voorhees and TE Ruth, "The Birthday: Lifeline or Deadline?" *Psychosomatic Medicine: Journal of Behavioral Medicine,* Volume 54, Issue 5, 1992.
[181] B Barraclough and D Shepherd, "Birthday Blues: the Association of Birthday with Self-Inflicted Death in the Elderly," *Acta Psychiatrica Scandinavica*, Volume 54, Issue 2, August, 1976.
[182] Brenda C. Coleman, "Having the Power to Postpone Death," Associated Press, April 11, 1990.
[183] H Royer and G Smith, "Can the Famous Really Postpone Death?" *Social Biology*, Fall-Winter Volume 45, 1998.

Chapter 4

Scientific Unintended Consequences

How Strength Leads to Weakness

Modern science helps people lead healthier more fulfilled lives. Scientific enquires have revealed layers of mystery about the human body and our environment. It is not surprising that people are most interested in scientific topics when they relate to their personal health. The level of knowledge possessed by patients about health matters has become so great that some doctors cringe when patients walk into their examining room with a notepad filled with scientific jargon and the results of recent studies gleaned from the Internet or the science columns of major newspapers People today have higher expectations about being healthy and are better informed about health matters than has ever been true in history.

Immunity, or the ability for a body to fight off infection or disease, resides at the core of the modern principles of healthy living. The modern scientific breakthrough with infectious diseases occurred in 1796 when Edward Jenner used cowpox virus to immunize people against the scourge of smallpox. Nearly 100 years later Jenner's work led to the development by Louis Pasteur of vaccination methods. Smallpox was a deadly killer. Over 80% of children and approximately 40% of adults succumbed to the disease once infected.[184] Though a healthy immune system is less dramatic an idea than a discovery that controls a disease like polio, maintaining and strengthening our personal immune system is widely believed to keep people healthy and disease free.

The common cold is an illness that affects every living person. Medically known as a viral upper respiratory tract infection (VURTI) the common cold is a highly contagious disease that afflicts adults 2 to 4 times per year on average and children between six and 12 times.[185] It has long been thought that persons with stronger immune systems would be less susceptible to infection with the common cold. Jennifer Ackerman recently pointed out the fallacy of this hypothesis.[186] She reports the results of an experiment in 1984 at the University of Copenhagen which found that individuals with severe cold symptoms had no more damage to their nasal tissues during the illness then after they recovered. Even more surprising she reports that cold symptoms can be created without cold viruses at all. The

---

[184] S Riedel, 2005, "Edward Jenner and the History of Smallpox and Vaccination, "*Proceedings (Baylor University Med Cent)* 18 (1): 21–5.
[185] Dr. Trisha Macnair, "The Common Cold," *bbc.co.uk Health*. BBC. http://www.bbc.co.uk/health/conditions/commoncold.shtml.
[186] Jennifer Ackerman, "How Not to Fight Colds," *The New York Times*, October 4, 2010.

symptoms result not from a viral infection but from the body's own production of inflammatory mediators. Moreover, she reports the results of another study that shows that one in four persons infected with the cold virus doesn't get sick.

Ackerman's conclusion is startling. In her own words,

"So susceptibility to cold symptoms is not a sign of a weakened immune system, but quite the opposite. And... to quell those symptoms, strengthening your immune system may be counterproductive."

What this means for personal health is that an unintended consequence of living a healthy lifestyle regime may be that the individual suffers from more cases of the common cold than do their less diligent and less healthy, counterparts.

This result is no less surprising than the recent discovery that by keeping our children and their environment too clean we may be causing them to become ill while young and later as adults. Thomas McDade a professor of anthropology at Northwestern University in a 2009 study wrote.

"Contrary to assumptions related to earlier studies, our research suggests that ultra-clean, ultra-hygienic environments early in life may contribute to higher levels of inflammation as an adult, which in turn increases risks for a wide range of diseases,"[187]

It is now believed that exposure to germs helps children to develop immunities and other responses that allow them to stave off allergies and asthma. In other words, parents who

---

[187] T. McDade, Julienne Rutherford; Linda Adair, and Christopher Kuzawa, 2009, "Early Origins of Inflammation: Microbial Exposures in Infancy Predict Lower Levels of C-reactive Protein in Adulthood," Proceedings of the Royal Society B: *Biological Sciences*.

maintain an overly clean and pristine environment by using anti-bacterial and microbial cleaning solutions may cause an unintended consequence that may later harm their children. Research at the Children's Hospital of Munich goes further and says that it is not just the number of germs children are exposed to but the variety of them that matters in making them healthier adults. [188] Children living on farms, for example, had a lower risk of developing asthma than did other children. The movement from farms to cities and the overuse of antibacterial agents may explain the doubling in the asthma rate in the US in the past 30 years.

Less than a century ago parents routinely deposited their children in the middle of the backyard dirt heap, a repository of any infinite variety of bacteria and viruses, and only cleaned them off late at night before dinner or going to bed. Yet the incidence of allergies and asthma in our super clean children is greater today than when there was less attention focused on cleanliness.

How Removing One Scourge Creates Another

Smallpox is an infectious disease that has been the bane of humankind since time immemorial. Evidence of smallpox appears on the body of Egyptian pharaohs and in writings from China and India 1,500 years before the millennium. Easily spread between people via airborne transmission of the virus, the disease has killed billions of humans. The 20th century death toll from smallpox is estimated at nearly ½ billion deaths. [189]

By vaccinating people around the world, smallpox became the first of two infectious diseases ever eradicated

---

[188] Shirley S Wang, "Germ Exposure Reduces Asthma Risk," *The New York Times*, February 23, 2011.
[189] David A Koplow, 2003, *Smallpox: the Fight to Eradicate a Global Scourge*. Berkeley: University of California Press.

(the other occurred in 2010 with the eradication of Rinderpest). The World Health Organization certified the eradication of smallpox in December 1979. Mankind had finally wiped out a deadly killer. The unintended consequence of this success has been the reemergence of monkeypox. Cases of monkeypox are now 20 times more common in the Congo then they were 30 years ago when the smallpox vaccination program was discontinued after its success.[190]

Like smallpox, monkeypox is an infectious disease caused by a virus. Last seen in the US in early 2000, the disease is less communicable than smallpox. Overall the rise of monkeypox and the demise of smallpox is a huge win for mankind. This unintended consequence is easy to accept because of the net gain. Moreover, risks associated with the smallpox vaccine itself are large enough to outweigh the gain from continued administration of the vaccine in order to control monkeypox.

How Removing One Scourge Creates Another: Part 2

This next unintended consequence could easily have fit into the human or government chapters. It wound up in the science chapter only because it has a simple scientific explanation. In 2010, an oil well being drilled by BP PLC exploded sending 5 million barrels of crude oil spewing into the Gulf of Mexico. This section is not about the accident but rather is about something that occurred as a result of this spill. Specifically, how the government tried to protect the fertile estuaries in Louisiana.

---

[190] Donald G. McNeill Jr., "Monkeypox Cases Surge in Rural Areas as Price of the Victory Over Smallpox," *The New York Times*, August 31, 2010.

Shortly after the oil spill, Louisiana officials opened gates in Mississippi River levees and sent fresh water to block oil filled salt water.[191] Reports suggest that the strategy worked to keep out much of the oil. The unintended consequence of this successful approach harmed oysters. Oysters require a specific water salinity to survive. Freshwater from the river mixed with salt water and changed its salinity. Some reports suggest that as many as 60% of the oysters died.[192] It is difficult to mess with science and not get an unintended consequence. Applying cost-benefit principles to this Louisiana situation is likely to reveal that the overall savings outweigh the costs borne by oyster fishermen.

How Saving Bambi Kills People

Who doesn't love a deer? Hikers spying these graceful animals in the woods stop in awe as do children visiting them at petting zoos. Walt Disney may have encouraged our affinity for this creature by his depiction of the plight of the orphaned Bambi in the eponymous film. Deer have been important to humankind throughout history. Not only has the animal's meat provided sustenance but its coat has been used for clothing and shoes and the animal has been a mode of transportation. Of course, few good things come without unintended consequences.

In the case of deer the two unintended consequences are automobile accidents with cars running into the animals and disease spread by ticks. The National Highway Traffic Safety Administration estimates that there are 1.5 million deer-vehicle collisions annually that result in approximately 150 human deaths. In addition, deer ticks spread illnesses such as Lyme disease when the tick moves from its deer host onto humans.

---

[191] Jeffrey Ball, "Dying Oysters Scourge: Fresh Water," *The Wall Street Journal*, July 20, 2010.
[192] Ibid.

The island of Nantucket offshore Massachusetts (and the site of many famous limericks) had no deer until 1922. [193] That was the year a fisherman saw a deer paddling in the ocean. The deer was rescued and brought to the island; later a mate was brought to the island out of pity for the deer's loneliness. Since then either love or biology has resulted in a massive increase in the deer population on the island. In 2008, there were 411 cases of tic borne illnesses on the island including Lyme disease, babesiosis and ehrlichiosis, the latter two of which can be fatal. In other words, the unintended consequence of someone's good behavior – rescuing a drowning deer - has led to a severe medical crisis on the island.

Further extending the crisis is the fact that deer are so cute. A deer hunt in 2005 which removed 246 deer from the island is unlikely to be repeated as resident's tradeoff the probability of contracting a tick borne disease against their personal unwillingness to kill the host. Pacifism concerning this furry animal neighbor who existence jeopardizes our health is probably an unintended consequence of the wonderful whimsy of the Disney film.

How Saving Bambi Injures Bambi

The last horse was slaughtered in an American abattoir in 2008. Many groups concerned about the humane treatment of animals worked together to achieve this outcome. Horsemeat had been used by zoos to feed carnivores and was exported to other countries for human consumption. While advocates were unable to get Congress to pass a law banning the slaughter of horses, animal rights groups did get Congress to stop funding for inspectors at

---

[193] Pam Belluck, "Tick Borne Illnesses have Nantucket Considering some Deer Based Solutions," *The New York Times*, September 6, 2009.

slaughterhouses; without an inspection the meat could not be exported thereby effectively ending the trade.[194]

Resonant of the tale about Bambi, advocates failed to consider what would happen to wild horses when the market ended for their meat at American slaughterhouses. Halting the slaughter of horses in the US did nothing to reduce the supply of unwanted animals. The first unintended consequence was that live horses were exported to Mexico for slaughter. Conditions in rail cars carrying the horses are abysmal and many animals suffer.

A second unintended consequence is that the US government is spending nearly $40 million a year to feed and house nearly 40,000 horses that had to be removed from the wild to avoid mass starvation amongst the herds. [195] It has been a long time since the US government slaughtered horses; it prefers a policy of adoption. However, horses breed too quickly and the population of wild horses continues to grow. During times of financial exigency, some question the logic of spending funds on horses that no one wants.

Many of the groups that had argued against slaughterhouses have reversed their positions and are now suggesting that abattoirs be reintroduced. At least these individuals are wise enough to recognize when unintended consequences change reality.

How Sexual Interest Depends on the Unexpected

If human sexuality can be extrapolated from the experience of rats then men who are raised in families with

---

[194] Stephanie Simon, "Horse Slaughter is Reconsidered," *The Wall Street Journal*, January 5, 2011.
[195] Ibid.

higher ratios of women grow up to have less interest in sex. A recent study in *Psychological Science* reports that male rats raised in an environment with six females and two males had fewer sexual encounters with ready and available females than did other rats raised in litters with two females and six males. [196] One explanation for this difference is that having a preponderance of females at home makes women less novel and therefore less enticing. [197]

Certain cultures favor male children to such an extent that they have used science to alter the normal sex mix of children using practices such as abortion and infanticide. The unintended consequence of this male-centric preference, inferring from rats, is a sexually supercharged male population. Having a bunch of Casanovas is not itself a problem and may be thought by some women to be advantageous. However, when the normal female/male sexual ratio is altered there are not a sufficient number of females for all these Casanovas. Unless prostitution is sanctioned for unmarried males those societies may confront greater frequencies of rape.

Society permits males to exercise with their shirt tops off while females must remain clothed. Perhaps society, who's main obligation is procreation, has known about the results of the rat study, and has endeavored to keep the male of the species from knowing too much about the female in either form or function. It may be that males too familiar with female nudity are less prone to sexual activity.

---

[196] Cynthia B. de Medeiros, Stephanie L. Rees, Maheleth Llinas, Alison S. Fleming and David Crews, 2010 "Deconstructing Early Life Experiences: Distinguishing the Contributions of Prenatal and Postnatal Factors to Adult Male Sexual Behavior in the Rat," *Psychological Science* (October).

[197] Christopher Shea, "Sisters vs. Sex," *The Wall Street Journal*, November 6, 2010.

How Sexual Interest Depends on the Unexpected: Part 2

Chemistry is important not just in the laboratory but also in the bedroom. [198] Women have used hormonal contraceptives since 1960. The pill acts upon a woman's endocrine system to prevent ovulation. Less well known is the fact that hormonal contraceptives also affect sexual attractiveness and sex drive.

Women taking hormonal contraceptives behave differently in sexual matters than other women. This unintended consequence has profound consequences for the happiness of couples. For example, women on contraceptives do not undergo a heightening of their interest in "masculine" man as do other women, during ovulation. [199] Moreover, the natural preference for men whose immune systems are the most different from their own breaks down when a woman is on hormonal contraceptives. The effect is not on women alone. Women not taking hormonal contraceptives are themselves more attractive to men when they ovulate.

Other changes in the sexual arena affect the female partner. For example, she is less interested in sex when on the pill - talk about an unintended consequence. Rather than creating a liberating opportunity for female sexual freedom, it appears that hormonal contraceptives may just provide men with willing partners who themselves have little interest in the act.

---

[198] Shirley S Wang, "The Tricky Chemistry of Attraction," *The Wall Street Journal*, May 9, 2011.
[199] Ibid.

How Antibiotic Use Can Be Bad

Antibiotics are among the scientific developments that have most extended human life. The work of Louis Pasteur and Fleming were cited earlier in this book. In 1939 Gerhard Domagk received the Nobel Prize in medicine for developing the first commercially available antibiotic while working at Bayer Laboratories. Prior to the advent of antibiotics people died from infections caused by cuts, airborne pathogens, and internal infections. Alexander the Great, for example, is said to have died from a scratch that led to an infection.

At first, doctors prescribed antibiotics too frequently and for too many ailments. Antibiotics were considered to be a wonder drug. Without data on the implications of their overuse, doctors prescribed antibiotics prophylactically against possible infection and to fight viral infections even though they are ineffective in that use. In some countries, antibiotics are sold over the counter allowing ill-informed individuals to easily misuse them. The unintended consequence of the advent of an overused miracle drug was the creation of drug resistant bacteria. Both penicillin and erythromycin, early antibiotics, experienced declining usefulness in fighting infections as early as the 1950s.

Sixty years later the problem is multi-antibiotic resistant bacteria. It is estimated that as many as 100,000 Americans die each year from infections acquired in hospitals for which there is no known antibiotic cure. The future may be direr. Diseases such as MRSA (methicillin-resistant *Staphylococcus aureus*,) or the recently discovered NDM-1 mutation, which allows bacteria to be invulnerable to most known antibiotics, have alarmed the medical profession. [200] Dr. Margaret Hamburg commissioner of the Food and Drug Administration said superbugs may again allow everyday infections to become mass killers. [201] The irony of this

---

[200] Andrew Pollack, 2010, "Looking for a Super Bug Killer," *The New York Times*, November 6, 2010.
[201] Ibid.

unintended consequence should not be lost on the reader. A good thing, in this case antibiotic, soon leads to a bad thing multi-antibiotic resistant bacteria,

Our food stock also confronts an antibiotic problem. For too long, farmers have prophylactically used antibiotics to protect livestock from infection. Antibiotics are regularly administered to cattle, pigs, and chicken thereby reducing the loss rate on farms. Although it's the same unintended consequence described above, animal products and wastes put antibiotics into our bodies and water systems thereby reducing the effectiveness of antibiotics. The simple answer is that an effort to control sickness among farm animals is responsible for human illnesses.

How Insecticide Use Can Be Bad

Efforts to control bedbugs have had a similar unintended consequence to the one described above for antibiotic use. Bedbugs are an annoying parasite that is more bothersome than fatal. They have troubled the human race for thousands of years especially with their fondness for inhabiting beds where humans sleep. Efforts to eradicate bedbugs have proved futile. Moreover, modern bedbugs have developed substantial resistance to pyrethroid the principal insecticide used against them. In fact, the dosage that would have killed bedbugs 10 years ago now must be increased a thousand fold to be effective. [202] The unintended consequence of trying to kill bed bugs has according to John Clark an insect toxicologist at the University of Massachusetts done, "nothing more than speed-up evolution."[203]

During the middle part of the 20th century the bedbug problem had been controlled to the point where their presence was unusual. Cockroaches, ants, and spiders are natural predators for bedbugs. Ironically, the unintended

---

[202] Robert Lee Hotz, "Rapidly Evolving Bedbugs Won't Die," *The Wall Street Journal*, January 20, 2011.
[203] Ibid.

consequence of the suppression of these predator insects from homes and hotels in the later part of the 20th century, as cleanliness and bug free environments became symbols of good housekeeping, may have unleashed of the current bedbug scourge bedeviling the hotel/motel industry worldwide.

How Natures Rhythms Cause Strange Dance Partners

As powerful as people might feel, compared to nature we are nothing. Jet airplanes carry us from one corner of the globe to another in less time than it takes some people to pack their bags. Nuclear power stations unleash the power of the sun to create nearly limitless electricity. Medical discoveries extend life expectancy by conquering diseases. But no matter how much we learn we must remain in awe of nature.

Nature affects us directly and indirectly through unintended consequences. An interesting example of an unintended consequence occurred in April 2010 with the eruption of the Eyjafjallajokull volcano in Iceland. The volcanoes discharge closed airspace over most European cities. One of those who trip was disrupted by the volcano was General Stanley McChrystal who was a four star general in the US army and who served as Commander, International Security Assistance Force and Commander, US Forces Afghanistan. General McChrystal and his staff were on their way to Berlin when their plane could not take off from Paris. Spending the week instead at the Ritz Carlton hotel in Paris, General McChrystal spent numerous hours with a *Rolling Stone* reporter named Michael Hastings.

During these conversations General McChrystal vented his frustrations with President Obama and the conduct of the war in Afghanistan. Perhaps these feelings would have come out anyway but the ash from the volcano put these two men together for an extended period of time and allowed them to develop a rapport that enabled the journalist to break through the normal shield protecting a high ranking military officer. The unintended consequence was that the president fired the general. The new commander General David Petraeus had previously commanded all troops fighting in Iraq. The conduct of the war changed hands as the result of a volcano thousands of miles away.

How Controlling One Medical Problem Fixes Another

The vaccine against human papillomavirus (HPV) is new and controversial. The virus on the other hand is ancient, varied in type (for most people the virus is asymptomatic), and can lead to genital warts or cancer in both genders. HPV is a sexually transmitted disease afflicting nearly 80% of sexually active individuals. [204] The virus is implicated in a variety of cancers in body locations specific to various sexual acts. Though it is not the sole cause of these cancers, control or eradication of HPV would limit incidents of these diseases.

In 2006 a new drug, Gardasil, was approved to prevent HPV infection. The vaccine was developed to help young women - the group it was tested upon. Young women are the only group sanctioned to receive the vaccine in most countries. The vaccine works by preventing new infections; it does nothing to limit existing infections. Some parent groups object to the vaccine and have refrained from giving it to their children for fear that it would encourage earlier sexual activity. This book ignores that topic.

Data showing that Gardasil prevents HPV infection are very strong. Despite its high cost, Gardasil will save thousands of lives. The unintended consequence of the administration of Gardasil to young women is a significant reduction in cases of HPV infection in young men. Australia

---

[204] "American Social Health Association - HPV Resource Center," 2007.

provides Gardasil for free to all female residents. [205]
Analyzing data on over 112,000 patients, researchers found
that after the wide administration of the vaccine, diagnoses
of genital warts declined by 59% among women and by 28%
among men. That is, even without administering the vaccine
to young man they still enjoyed some of the benefits as a
result of the vaccination program in young women. A study
at the Harvard Medical School concluded that it may not be
cost effective to administer the vaccine in young males
provided that it is administered to young women.[206]

How Abstinence from Alcohol may be Harmful

The consumption of alcohol began during prehistory.
Presumably the earliest alcoholic beverages were obtained
by fermentation of sugars occurring in plants, such as beer or
mead, rather than by a distillation process, such as vodka or
gin. Whatever its form, in many places alcohol consumption
is widespread and associated with sporting events and
communal activities. Judaism and Christianity include
alcohol in their religious ceremonies while Islam, Buddhism,
Mormonism and Hinduism require adherents to maintain
strict abstinence. Religious opposition to alcohol
consumption is due partially to problems associated with
alcohol: including alcoholism and drunk driving.

At various times and in various places the complete
prohibition of alcohol consumption has been enforced. In the
US prohibition was enacted with the 18th amendment to the
Constitution and lasted for 13 years from 1920 - 1933. The
unintended consequences of governmental prohibition of

---

[205] Sexually Transmitted Infections, The Research Report, *The Wall Street Journal*, November 17, 2010.

[206] Jane J Kim and Sue J Goldie, "Cost Effectiveness Analysis of Including Boys in a Human Papillomavirus Vaccination Program in the United States," *BMJ*, 2009; 339: B3884.

any substance are discussed in Chapter 2 of this book. The rise of organized crime and the illegal production and importation of alcohol during prohibition is widely known. Al Capone and Lucky Luciano, infamous characters from this period, are names recognized worldwide. The vast majority of Americans celebrated the repeal of the 18th amendment; though some states and municipalities continued to ban alcohol following 1933.

A famous advocate of alcohol prohibition is the Women's Christian Temperance Union (WCTU). The WCTU actively campaigned and crusaded for prohibition. Its message clearly resonated across the land as the organization's membership grew from 20,000 in 1881 to more than 370,000 in 1931. Its most famous leader was Frances Willard an ardent speaker and advocate of abstinence. The town of Evanston Illinois where the WCTU is headquartered remained dry until 1972. The message of the WCTU and Frances Willard was that an abstinent life promoted a healthy life.

Many people believed the health claims of anti-alcohol advocates. On the one hand was presented an alcoholic father who beat and abused his children while losing his job and the family's home; while on the other hand you had a teetotaler father who beamed his familial love all day and who was a good breadwinner to boot. Most people now believe that the average person can consume a moderate amount of alcohol and control their urges and remain an upstanding member of society.

The unintended consequence of the alcohol abstinence message is that it disregards the positive health benefits of alcohol consumption. There are significant health benefits for both men and women from the moderate consumption of alcohol. For example, men consuming three or more alcoholic beverages a week were found to have a

35% lower risk of heart attack[207]; adults over 55 consuming 1 to 3 drinks a day have a 42% lower risk of dementia[208]; and the chemical resveratrol which is found in red wine may have anti-cancer properties, may lengthen life expectancy, and may protect the cardiovascular system. The Harvard Medical School examined 200,000 women and found that women consuming up to two drinks a day were healthier in old-age. [209] It also concluded that women had a 28% increase in their chance of successfully surviving to the age of 70 if they consumed one or two drinks a day. [210]

This is a strange unintended consequence. Not only was it totally unexpected just several decades ago but it runs counter to intuition and the long believed popular view that doing something that you enjoy cannot be good for you. People who listened to the inaccurate message of teetotalers may have suffered health consequences.

How Prudence Is Imprudent

One of the strangest unintended consequences arises from what economists call "the paradox of thrift." The modern proponent of this paradox was the British economist John Maynard Keynes who described the idea that if everyone in a country tries to save more money then in fact everyone will save less. That is, the unintended consequence of a predisposition in a society to save more results in a reduction in aggregate savings: trying to save more results in less being saved.

The great economic crisis which began in December 2007 and which officially ended in June 2009 created a wish

[207] "Frequent Tipple Cuts Heart Risk," BBC News. 2008-01-09.
[208] Alcohol Could Reduce Dementia Risk,'" BBC News. 2002-01-25.
[209] Jennifer Corbett Dooren, "Ok to Make That a Double, Study Finds, *The Wall Street Journal*, November 16, 2010 November 16, 2010.
[210] ibid.

to deleverage (i.e., owe less money) among individuals, companies and governments. Deleveraging is a process. It reduces current indebtedness and uses less debt in future endeavors. Deleveraging is achieved by saving out of income. In other words, a decision by people, companies and governments to deleverage requires them to spend less and save more.

The recessionary period from 2007 - 2009 was one of the most severe and damaging perhaps since the economic depression of the 1930s. Psychologically the impact on all participants has been profound. The most regrettable truth about the recent economic crisis is that the economy has failed to grow sufficiently to create jobs to reemploy millions of workers. There are many explanations for the stagnant economy, but a key one is the unintended consequence caused by the paradox of thrift. People who borrowed money throughout their lives now try to live prudently; governments and corporations have done the same.

As these agents work to reduce their indebtedness, the unintended consequence of the paradox of thrift kicks in. Since there is more saving and less spending, the aggregate demand for goods and services declines leading to a loss in jobs, income, and savings. While specific individuals may increase their absolute dollar savings, aggregate savings decline as a result of there being fewer jobs generating lower income. This happens even though everyone in society increases their average savings rate. But when a higher percentage savings rate is applied to a lower national income level, total aggregate savings decline.

How National Altruism can be Excessive

Government tax and spending policies have unintended consequences. In our society, the social safety net (programs that provide needy people with cash, food, healthcare, and other needs) and government-funded or supported programs (such as Social Security, Medicare, and Medicaid) have transitioned from supplying basic needs to providing them generous levels of support.

The US government's budget is severely out of balance. Which programs are responsible for the deficit? In most countries social safety net programs are just 1 - 2% of GDP. [211] That amount of altruism is unlikely to create budgetary problems. On the other hand, nondiscretionary spending consumes vast portions of the federal government's budget; Social Security was 20% of federal spending in fiscal year 2009, Medicare and Medicaid combined for a further 19%, while an additional 17% of the federal budget is classified as mandatory spending. In the aggregate, over 50% of government spending is earmarked for programs that are arguably altruistic. The question is how much altruism can a society afford? The quote heard in a short snippet from a TV news broadcast about a Tea Party rally was "stop government spending but keep your hands off my Medicare," shows how delicate is the question of what is appropriate government spending.

Suppose the federal government behaved like a family would upon discovering that their spending vastly outpaces their income. Most likely, the family would seek ways to supplement their income, with second jobs or gifts from family members, and would reduce spending. With a carefully planned retrenchment a family might regain solvency and avoid further financial embarrassment. Now suppose that the federal government behaved similarly. The government would raise taxes and reduced spending. While the family's actions yielded positive benefits, a similar program by the federal government could create a disaster because of unintended consequences.

---

[211] Grosh M, del Ninno C, & Tesliuc E, 2008, "For Protection and Promotion: The Design and Implementation of Effective Safety Nets," Washington DC: The World Bank.

Though not all economists accept the Keynesian model, it argues that both tax increases and lower government spending <u>reduce</u> national output, income, and jobs. What works for a family does not work for government. Governmental efforts by to balance its budget have the unintended consequence of causing an economic slowdown. This handicaps a government attempting to reestablish fiscal control. It either allows the deficit to continue or it takes action which slows the economy.

How did the US get here? How can a great country be unable to balance its budget? The answer may be unpopular because it concerns how much benevolence a society can extend to the less fortunate. Unquestionably incomes are unequal in the US but the less well-off are far better off in an absolute scale than they were 10, 20, or 30 years ago. The question is when is enough enough?

My son Jesse told me a story he heard in a lecture given by Steven Levitt the University of Chicago economist and author of the book *Freakonomics*. Leavitt said that a company owner after a very good year gave each of his employees a frozen turkey during the holiday season. The employees were so grateful that they couldn't stop thanking their benefactor and worked extra hard right after the holiday season ended. The next year the employer had another good business year and again provided his employees with the turkey; this time fewer employees thanked him and productivity didn't change. The following year was not a good one for the business and to save funds the employer did not give his employees a turkey. Not only was he not thanked, but virtually every employee asked him where their turkey was? The moral of this story of course is that people come to expect what they have been given. In other words, the unintended consequence of giving a gift is that people expect you to continue giving them gifts. It is very hard if not impossible for government programs once offered to be retracted. Given that reality, it is easy to understand how more than half of the federal budget has become nondiscretionary.

Too few politicians know about Hauser's Law. [212] Hauser noted that over the past six decades regardless of the tax rate, the total tax take of the federal government has equaled approximately 19% of GDP. Over this period, tax rates on the highest earners in the US have ranged from 28% (in 1988 -1990) to 92% (in 1952 -1953). After adjusting the tax schedules, the federal government has not been able to influence the share of GDP that it gets. Hauser's message then is that since the government is going to receive 19% of GDP it would be better off if GDP were larger. Raising taxes, as seen above, does not increase GDP but decreases it. It seems that the way to balance the budget is to reduce spending or to accelerate growth.

How Good Becomes Better But Sometimes Worse

In all of science there is practically nothing as simple or as wonderful as acetylsalicylic acid otherwise known as aspirin. A product of willow bark, aspirin-like medications have been available since antiquity. First marketed in 1899 by Bayer AG the drug is now available worldwide, in numerous forms, and at low prices. Not only is aspirin used for pain relief but just as its sales felt competition from ibuprofen its anti-adhesive effects on blood platelets was discovered creating a new market for aspirin as a drug to prevent heart attacks and strokes.

Aspirin fits this book perfectly. Its use causes both positive and negative unintended consequences. A negative aspect of aspirin use is that it can lead to gastrointestinal bleeding. Like potato chips, aspirin is easily overused. By that

---

[212] W Kurt Hauser, "There's No Escaping Hauser's Law, *The Wall Street Journal*, November 26, 2010.

I mean it is very hard to take just a few potato chips or to limit one's use of aspirin when pain or fever flares. The body can only tolerate so much acetylsalicylic acid. In fact, the discovery of aspirin's anti-adhesive effects on blood platelets occurred in 1950 when a family doctor, Dr. Lawrence Craven, prescribed aspirin gum for his patients who had just had tonsillectomies. Dr. Craven observed that the gum was effective in reducing the pain associated with tonsillectomies but also that patients who consumed excessive amounts of the gum had to be hospitalized for internal bleeding.[213] The balance when using aspirin is very delicate: use too little and the pain doesn't go away, use too much and bleed internally.

Another negative unintended consequence of aspirin occurs when it is used by children and adolescents. This population runs the risk of contracting Reye's syndrome if aspirin is used to relieve fever or infection which can affect either their brain or liver. Again the delicate balance of who should use aspirin must be considered before dispensing it.

Aspirin is like that bunny promoting a long-life battery or, for those readers who go way back, like a Timex watch that John Cameron Swayze said "keeps on ticking." Every time that aspirin's popularity and sales wane a new positive unintended consequence resuscitates it. Most recently, it has been shown that people taking baby aspirins once a day for the positive health benefits of reduced heart attacks and strokes were in addition 21% less likely to die of solid tumor cancers including those in the stomach, esophagus, and lung.[214] It's unlikely that aspirin use will diminish, in the aggregate, any time soon.

---

[213] J Miner and A Hoffhines, 2007, "The Discovery of Aspirin's Antithrombotic Effects," *Texas Heart Institute Journal* 34 (2): 179–86.
[214] Roni Caryn Rabin, "Aspirin Helps in Reducing Cancer Deaths, a Study Finds," *The New York Times*, December 7, 2010.

How a Rose is not a Rose When it comes to Red Meat

Meat played a less prominent role in a typical family's diet 100 years ago.[215] On a per capita basis, in 1909 approximately 210 pounds of meat were consumed. This has increased to more than 300 pounds today. Health advocates associate increased meat consumption with a corresponding increase in the death rate from cardiovascular disease. From 1900 to 1975 the death rate from cardiovascular-renal disease increased by nearly 50%.[216] Since then medical technology and greater health awareness have reduced the cardiovascular death rate.

In 1900 refrigeration was not available in the typical American home (central power stations began producing electricity in 1881 but the cost was prohibitive to the average family). Instead, people used pantries with marble shelves to preserve food. They also shopped daily for food and had fewer perishable leftovers. Foods that pickled, canned, or jellied were preferred because they were longer-lived. Technology came to the rescue with artificial food additives designed to extend the lives of food items. Examples include sodium nitrate, sodium nitrite, sulfites, and disodium EDTA. With this technological change families reduced their shopping trips and kept food in the refrigerator longer.

Processed meats in particular are heavy users of artificial food additives. Hot dogs, salami, sausage links, baloney, bacon, corned beef, and pastrami are all familiar names to the American consumer. Some people consume

---

[215] Gerrior S. and Bente, L. "Selected Food and Nutrient Highlights of the 20th Century: US Food Supply Series," *Family Economics and Nutrition Review* Vol. 14, No 1, 2002. Also see Amrock J., "Causes and Effects of the Changing American Diet: 1900 to the Present," March 25, 2003.
[216] Ibid, Amrock.

processed meats at every meal. The unintended consequence of finding a scientific solution to reduce food spoilage may be the dramatic rise in cardiovascular disease. A recent study by the Harvard School of Public Health notes that a daily diet of 4 ounces of non-processed red meat was not associated with any increase in cardiovascular disease.[217] In contrast, the mere consumption of 2 ounces a day of processed meats created a 42% increase in the risk of heart disease.[218]

On the one hand the lack of food preservation systems resulted in deaths from bacterial illnesses such as salmonella, Campylobacter jejuni, and Escherichia coli O157:H7 not to mention viral or parasitic ailments. On the other hand, the technologically-based solution to the food preservation problem appears to have contributed to a higher cardiovascular death rate.

How Wealth Creates Myopia

Computers, TVs, schoolwork, video games, and other distractions that keep children indoors rather than playing outside has a surprising unintended consequence. In the past 40 years the proportion of children diagnosed with nearsightedness has increased significantly. In the US the nearsightedness percentage has jumped from 25% in the 1970s to 42% in 2011.[219] Lack of outdoor activity may be the principal contributor to this phenomenon. An Asian study comparing children of Chinese extraction living in Sydney Australia to those living in Singapore found a nine times

---

[217] Ron Winslow, "A Guilt Free Hamburger," *The Wall Street Journal*, May 18, D1. 2011.

[218] Micha, R., Wallace S K, and Mozaffarian, D., "Red and Processed Meat Consumption and Risk of Incident Coronary Heart Disease, Stroke, and Diabetes Mellitus: A Systematic Review and Meta-Analysis" *Circulation.* 2010 Jun 1;121(21):2271-83. Epub 2010 May 17.

[219] Aamondt, S. and S. Wang, "The Sun is the Best Optometrist," *The New York Times*, June 21, 2011.

higher rate of nearsightedness among those in Singapore than in Sydney. [220] Children in Sydney were outside for approximately 14 hours per week while those in Singapore spent just three hours per week outdoors.

The science of myopia, nearsightedness, is relatively simple. Eyes become nearsighted when too long a distance develops between the lens and the retina. [221] It is theorized that exposure to bright sunlight helps children's eyes to maintain the correct lens and retina distance. [222] By achieving a higher standard of living, our children face the unintended consequence of not being able to see long distances. The simple remedy of asking children to engage in their high-tech lifestyle outdoors doesn't work because of the way sunlight affects screens on handheld computer devices.

How Being Green May Actually Be Black

Biofuels and other forms of sustainable energy may someday be the salvation of mankind. Until then caution needs to be exercised in how rapidly nontraditional forms of energy are adopted. Biofuel is derived from solid, liquid or gaseous biomass. The logic to biofuels is elegant: plants absorb carbon dioxide as they grow which balances carbon dioxide released when they are burned. Theoretically they have a zero balance - the perfect fuel. [223]

The European Community group adopted palm oil as a substitute for hydrocarbons. Their rush to sustainable

---

[220] Ferrari J. and L. Hall, TheAustralian.news.com.au, January 6, 2009.

[221] Aamodt and Wang op. cit.

[222] Ibid, Aamodt and Wang explain that engaging in the near work, such as needlepoint or jewelry making, is not responsible for the development of nearsightedness.

[223] Elizabeth Rosenthal, "Once a Dream Fuel, Palm Oil May Be an Eco--Nightmare," *The New York Times*, January 31, 2007

energy with biofuels required government subsidies and the redesign of their energy infrastructure. [224] These plans may have reduced emissions if palm oil producers had not responded to market signals by creating an environmental unintended consequence.

When profits are earned and prices rise producers increase their output. Any other response would be illogical. Increased production of palm oil required the destruction of parts of the Southeast Asian rainforest, excessive use of chemical fertilizers, and the burning of large tracts of peat. Rainforest destruction reduces the absorption of carbon dioxide by living plant matter; chemical fertilizer runoff pollutes the ocean and promotes the growth of algae and the loss of normal life forms; and peat burning turned Indonesia into the third leading producer of carbon emissions. [225]

Unintended consequences made a transition to biofuels in Europe a mistake. Other scientists propose moving to second-generation biofuels. [226] One advantage is that this would take pressure off of food crops such as corn which are used to make ethanol. Non-food alternatives include reeds and wild grasses. However, other scientists warn of unintended consequences from these natural agents which are weeds that may spread to areas outside of bio farms.

Further exasperating the quest for a green or sustainable world is something that energy economists refer to as the "rebound effect. "[227] The rebound effect arises for example when a consumer buys a more fuel-efficient air-conditioner, uses it more frequently, and thereby actually increases energy consumption. On the one hand, the

---

[224] Ibid.

[225] Ibid.

[226] Elisabeth Rosenthal, "New Trend in Biofuels Carries New Risks," *The New York Times*, May 21, 2008.

[227] John Tierney, "When Energy Efficiency Sullies the Environment," *The New York Times*, March 8, 2011.

consumer is better off with a cheaper way to cool their house; on the other hand, the investment in greater energy efficiency by manufacturers actually may result in more energy use. Rebound effects are real as documented in a study by Jeff Tsao who found that the advent of LED lighting technology rather than reducing energy consumption will drive people to light up more parts of their home thereby increasing energy consumption.[228] Increased consumption is an unintended consequence of making energy use less costly via energy-saving technologies. There's nothing wrong with people deciding to leave the lights on in their basement, for example, after switching to an energy-saving bulb. But this paradoxical response, caused by an unintended consequence, may easily negate any benefit derived from new technology.

How the Pursuit of Science Can be Harmful

Penguins, the flightless birds of Antarctica, are appealing animals whose lifestyles have been chronicled in cartoon movies and on TV. Scientists have an interest in the migratory habits of penguins. In order to track their movement scientist have banded them with metal bracelets attached to either their legs or flippers. Banding is a common scientific technique to enable identification of migratory animals.

Unfortunately, in the case of penguins relative to overall body weight the steel rings are too heavy.[229] The unintended consequence has been that scientists have harmed their subjects. A ten-year study found that survival

---

[228] Jeff Tsao, "Solid-State Lighting: An Energy Economics Perspective," *Journal of Physics*, D 43 354001, 2010.
[229] *Daily Mail Reporter*, "Penguins Tagged by Scientist with Metal Bands 'Die More Quickly and Have Fewer Chicks." January 13, 2011.

rates of banded birds were 44% lower than non-banded birds. Apparently, the extra weight wore the birds out as they foraged for food making them susceptible to predators and illness. Moreover, banded birds gave birth to 41% fewer chicks. Overall, the subjects of this scientific experiment would have been better off being left alone.

How the Pursuit of Science Can be Harmful: Part 2

Amateur scientists/tourists flock to ecotourism parks in Africa to share the life pattern of mountain gorillas. [230] With fewer than 800 of these majestic creatures alive, there is a heightened interest in seeing for oneself how they live and in taking steps to protect them. Ecotourism, which is thought to be a sustainable activity, creates parks as self-supporting wildlife sanctuaries. Tourist dollars boost the local economy.

Autopsies of the two most recent guerrilla deaths revealed that the compassion of humans has had an unfortunate unintended consequence. Both deaths were caused by a human virus that was transmitted across species as a result of close contact between the apes and people. Short of requiring tourist to wear respirators, it would seem that the mountain gorilla's existence must remain lonely and separate from that of humans.

How a Tragic Story Can Have a Happy Ending

Thalidomide is a drug responsible for tens of thousands of heartbreaking birth defects. It was prescribed from 1957 through 1961 as a way to reduce the morning

---

[230] Grist, "A Lethal Sneeze," *The New York Times*, April 2, 2011.

sickness of pregnant women. Many children whose mothers took the drug were born with phocomelia, a disorder resulting in the underdevelopment of parts of their body such as limbs, ears, and noses. Despite the tragic nature of thalidomide its introduction has had two positive unintended consequences. The first was that after the tragedy most countries began to require strict safety testing of new drugs before they permitted licensure. The experiences of these unfortunate children suffering as a result of thalidomide have saved countless others.

The second unintended consequence resulting from the thalidomide disaster was that scientists explored alternative uses for the compound because of its very strong chemical activity. The drug has recently been used as part of a treatment for multiple myeloma and to control pain in patients with severe leprosy. Fears about misuse of the drug remain high and scientists have sought alternatives to its use whenever possible.

These benefits or unintended consequences are similar to the recent discovery that stem cells, which are transformable into specialized cell types, can be artificially grown in the laboratory. Research to find alternative means to produce stem cells arose as a result of a US government restriction against the use of embryonic stem cell lines. While it is far too early to predict, it is conceivable that the unintended consequence of being able to produce stem cells in the laboratory will lead to other important medical scientific breakthroughs.

How a Happy Story Can Have a Tragic Ending

Infertility is a terrible problem that affects both sexes. Approximately 15% of all couples have one infertile partner with men accounting for approximately 25% and women for about 50% of the cases (the remaining 1/4 of cases cannot be attributed). Although some cases of infertility cannot be treated, modern science has made tremendous headway with assorted assisted reproductive technologies (ART). The most common is in vitro fertilization (IVF) where an egg and sperm meet outside the female's body. Other ART techniques include artificial insemination and reproductive surgery.

Nearly 200,000 couples employee IVF treatment each year. The success rate for the procedure depends upon the woman's age. For women under thirty-five nearly 1/3rd have a live birth. For women over forty, the success rate per IVF cycle is less than 10%. The cost for an IVF cycle is approximately $20,000 a high figure but a small fraction of the total lifetime cost of raising a child. For couples struggling to have children, and whose IVF treatment is not paid for by insurance, this is probably the best money they have ever spent. IVF treatment is one of the great miracles of modern science.

The unintended consequence of in vitro fertilization is a higher risk of birth defects. Over 6% of IVF babies had major birth defects a rate approximately 50% higher than for naturally conceived children. [231] Many of these problems occur because of the higher rate of preterm birth amongst IVF children.

A second unintended consequence of IVF treatment is a vastly higher rate of multiple births. Twins now account for 3% of all births which is 70% higher than it had been in 1980. Most of these cases involved IVF. [232] One problem with multiple births is that they are associated with a higher rate of preterm babies and have greater long-term health issues.

---

[231] Olson CK, Keppler-Noreuil KM, Romitti PA, Budelier WT, Ryan G, Sparks AE, Van Voorhis BJ (2005). "In Vitro Fertilization is Associated with an Increase in Major Birth Defects". *Fertil Steril* 84 (5): 1308–15.
[232] Laurie Tarkan, "Lowering Odds of Multiple Births," *The New York Times*, February 19, 2008.

Multiple births occur because more than one embryo is transferred during the IVF treatment because of the low success rate with just a single embryo. The need for early success is predicated both on the cost of the procedure and on the age of the women.

Most couples receiving ART treatment have no problems and are overjoyed by the outcome; but the two unintended consequences have led to disappointment and sadness amongst a small segment of the affected population.

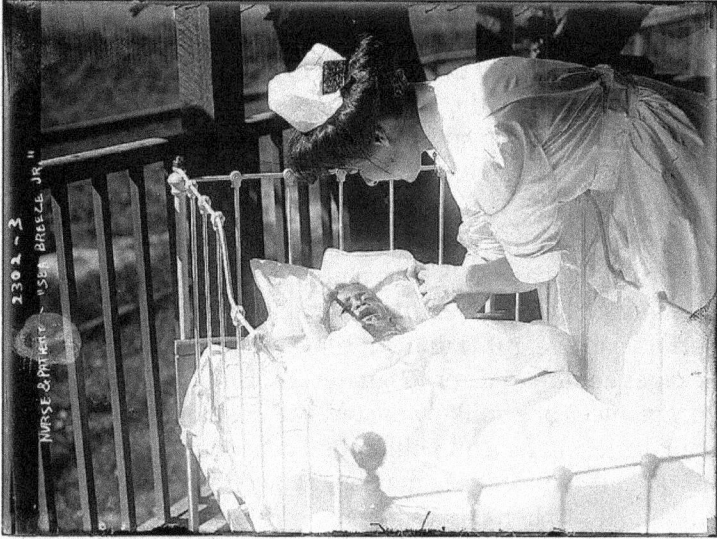

Chapter 5

Technological Unintended Consequences

How Good and Bad Balance Out

Technology is wonderful. Life as we know it would be impossible without computers. We buy airline tickets online and go to the airport where we swipe a credit card and then board a plane; the National Oceanic and Atmospheric Administration uses large supercomputers to predict the weather; and pharmaceutical companies are developing drugs based on a person's DNA sequence. But sometimes technology has unintended consequences.

Overnight worldwide package delivery is miraculous. Companies like FedEx and UPS rely on technology including computers, logistics models (e.g., hub and spoke systems), and jet aircraft to get packages half-way around the world overnight. Following the tradition of the Pony Express which delivered mail from the East to the West Coast in just 10 days, these companies transport packages from one part of the world to another. An unintended consequence of this wonder occurred in early November 2010: package bombs were sent via overnight couriers from the Middle East to Europe and America. FedEx and UPS both ship more than three million packages a day. With nearly three billion packages shipped by couriers each year it is difficult to be certain that none of the packages contain dangerous materials. Unintended consequences are unlikely to slow the development of technologies. In fact, an unintended consequence of this unintended consequence may be the acceleration of new technologies to better screen packages for hidden explosives.

How Modern Conveniences Bring Destruction

The world that we know in all of its complexity actually has some very simple structural associations. For example, an entrepreneur or an inventor perceives a need and creates a product that is quickly brought to market bringing riches to the business venture and breathtaking convenience to the consumer.

However, in the sprint to design, develop, and commercialize a new product little effort is devoted to its possible unintended consequences; in part this neglect is related to the fact that problems, if they exist, may not surface for decades if in fact they ever do. Worse still, some of these technological advances incorporate such sophisticated science including chemistry, physics, and engineering that they may cause fundamental changes in and unintended consequences upon the human body. Two examples of these unintended consequences are a recently discovered link between attention-deficit hyperactivity disorder (ADHD) and pesticides and a postulated and widely believed link between bisphenol A (BPA) and a host of ailments including obesity, cancer, reproductive system failure and neurological disorders.

Pesticides are compounds which either kill or repel pests including plants, insects, and rodents. Pesticide use is widespread in agriculture despite it being highly toxic. The most dangerous chemicals in the world are pesticides.[233] Yet farmers have used pesticides for thousands of years. Early farmers lacking knowledge in organic chemistry used dangerous compounds such as sulfur, arsenic, and nicotine as pesticides. Arsenic based pesticides were not supplanted until the 1950s when DDT was discovered. This miracle compound, DDT, itself had an unintended consequence that was revealed in the book *Silent Spring* by Rachel Carson. She described how DDT affected the reproductive cycle of birds. It became an early clarion call to environmentalists and the organic farming movement. Since the 1950s, agricultural and home use of pesticides has grown by more than 50 times.[234] A growing number of pesticides are in use. An insufficient amount of research has gone into the study of the long-term safety of pesticides.

ADHD is a psychiatric disorder usually first diagnosed in children. As the name implies, ADHD afflicted patients experience both attentional problems and hyperactivity. Although ADHD is not a new ailment its incidence is increasing. A 1998 study by the National Institutes of Health concluded that ADHD is a valid disorder, appears to afflict between 3 and 5% of school age children, and is 5 to 10 times more likely in the US then in other countries.[235] A few

---

[233] Gilden RC K Huffling, and B Sattler, 2010, "Pesticides and Health Risks," *Journal of Obstetrics and Gynecology and Neonatal Nursing* 39 (1): 103–10, January.

[234] Miller, GT, 2002, *Living in the Environment*, 12th Ed., Belmont: Wadsworth/Thomson Learning.

[235] National Institutes of Health, Consensus Statement on the Diagnosis and Treatment of ADHD, NIH Consensus Statement. 1998, 16:1-37.

observers contend that some diagnoses of ADHD are politically correct explanations for bad behavior that skirt more obvious links such as absentee parents or inferior educational systems. Others contend that environmental factors including heavy metals, PCBs, phenols, pesticides, or vaccines are responsible for a growing rate ADHD in our children. [236]

Some of the controversy about the causes of ADHD evaporated recently with the publication of a study in the journal *Pediatrics*. [237] Using US health data the authors linked childhood pesticide exposure to ADHD. The team of researchers from the University of Montreal and Harvard University found a 35% increase in the probability that a child would develop ADHD for every 10 fold increase in the child's concentration of urinary pesticide residue. A related study at Emory University in 2008 found that children who stopped eating pesticide-laced fruits and vegetables and who switched to organic foods had their concentration of urinary pesticide residue drop to negligible levels. [238] Children with above average concentration of urinary pesticide residue had a 20% incident of ADHD while those with negligible concentration of urinary pesticide residue had a 10% ADHD incidence level.

Scientific studies cannot always prove the connection between cause and effect. In the case of ADHD and pesticides the true culprit maybe other factors that are not part of the study. But until further research uncovers these other factor it is reasonable to argue that pesticides whose usage contributed to the Green Revolution in food production and that helped alleviate hunger throughout the world may have

---

[236] A not too dissimilar view is held regarding autism another childhood malady whose diagnoses have increased dramatically.

[237] Maryse F. Bouchard, David C. Bellinger, Robert O. Wright,, and Marc G. Weisskopf, 2010, "Attention-Deficit/Hyperactivity Disorder and Urinary Metabolites of Organophosphate Pesticides," *Pediatrics*, May 17, 2010.

[238] Associated Press, "Study Sees ADHD-Pesticide Link," *The Wall Street Journal*, May 18, 2010.

an equally nasty unintended consequence: causing an epidemic of children who suffer from ADHD. The inability to concentrate, to sit still, and to avoid distraction so common to ADHD sufferers makes these children's future far more difficult than their non-afflicted peers.

The second unintended consequence in this section relates to a chemical compound commonly referred to as BPA. BPA is used in the production of polycarbonate plastics, the clear shatterproof material used to make baby bottles, sports bottles, dental fillings, and other everyday products. BPA is one of those chemical compounds that make life easier. Is BPA essential? Of course not. But in the modern world it is omnipresent. Until recently avoiding BPA was nearly impossible.

Scientific research has demonstrated that BPA is an endocrine disruptor that acts like natural hormones in the body. A large body of research has found an association between BPA and a wide variety of ailments. Little research if any has exonerated BPA. A study in the *Journal of the American Medical Association* on humans found a significant association between BPA levels and heart disease and diabetes.[239] Animal studies describe a nearly endless array of medical problems associated with BPA levels: changes in breast cells, changes in prostates, neurological effects, among others. BPA is less important to the world than are pesticides. Other plastics can replace BPA albeit with less functionality. Moving agriculture to an organic state is a far greater endeavor. That may explain why manufacturers have so quickly moved to drop BPA from their products while worldwide usage of pesticides continues to grow.

The problem with unintended consequences is that their damages may not appear immediately but instead may lurk in the shadows for decades or else are missed altogether because of other false or misleading associations. That's what

---

[239] Lang IA, Galloway TS, Scarlett A, Henley WE, Depledge M, Wallace RB, Melzer D, 2008, "Association of Urinary Bisphenol A Concentration with Medical Disorders and Laboratory Abnormalities in Adults," *JAMA* 300 (300): 1303.

makes unintended consequences such a tricky subject. On the one hand it could be argued that no technological progress should be permitted because deep within its bowels may reside a problem that will surface in the future; obviously that is not a good solution. Alternately, it could be argued that unintended consequences from technological progress should be ignored because they probably don't exist and even if they do they may not surface for a long time; obviously that is not a good solution either. Somewhere in the middle of these two extremes rests a middle ground that will permit technological progress but at the same time will provide protection from its unintended consequences.

How Removing One Bad May Lead to a Bigger Bad

Few things taste better than strawberries. Cut up and put on cereal, in a bowl with cream, or made into jelly or preserves, the garden strawberry is loved. Strawberry plants are prone to diseases of its leaves, roots, and fruit. While most strawberry farmers still pick the fruit by hand, they also tend to liberally use pesticides to protect their crop. Organic farming of strawberries is increasing in part because studies show that the organic variety have more taste, anti oxidants and vitamin C than conventionally grown strawberries though they tend to be smaller and have less potassium and phosphorus. [240] But the vast majority of strawberries are still grown using heavy doses of pesticides.

Over 90% of strawberries grown in the US come from California. [241] Those farmers tend to incorporate pesticide use in their agriculture. The principle chemical used for

---

[240] Karen Kaplan, "Organic Strawberries are better-in Some Ways-Researchers Say," *Los Angeles Times*, September 2, 2010.
[241] Malia Wollan, "Dispute over Pesticide for California Strawberries has Implications Beyond State," *The* New York Times, June 19, 2010.

strawberry farming was methyl bromide. [242] That abruptly stopped when the Montreal Protocol banned methyl bromide as an ozone depletor. Good science had come to the rescue. Ozone depletion from the atmosphere has occurred at a fairly steady 4% rate since 1970. Reduction in ozone leads to an increase in the amount of ultraviolet radiation reaching the earth. Banning ozone depleting chemicals is science working to protect the atmosphere.

The unintended consequence of this good scientific research occurred because strawberry farmers were unwilling to convert to organic farming methods. Instead, they looked for a new pesticide to replace methyl bromide. Methyl iodide seemed to fit the bill; it is less harmful to the ozone and still protects the strawberry crop. It was approved for agricultural use by Federal regulators in 2007. [243] Some scientists however are not sure that the decision was a good one. Theodore Slotkin, a Duke University medical school professor of pharmacology and cancer biology said, "[it] is known to be neurotoxic, as well as developmentally toxic and an endocrine disruptor..."[244] While John Froines, a professor of environmental health science at UCLA said "this is without question one of the most toxic chemicals on earth."[245]

If these scientists are right then the unintended consequence of protecting the ozone layer may be that we have permitted a chemical, methyl iodide, which will contribute to what Dr. Slotkin calls a silent pandemic of learning disabilities, autism, and ADHD disorder. [246] The calculus is intriguing. If ozone depletion leads to higher cancer rates while autism and other disorders lead to dysfunctional children, how does it balance out?

---

[242] ibid.
[243] ibid.
[244] ibid.
[245] ibid.
[246] ibid.

How Phoning Home May Cause Death

Ask anyone under the age of 30 which modern convenience would be the last one they would give up, and most would say their cell phone. There are now 292 million wireless phones in use in the US with which Americans make 2.26 trillion minutes (about 10,000 per person) of cell phone calls annually. [247] The first handheld cellular phone was created in 1973 and the first commercial cell phone was sold in 1983. To go from no users to almost one phone per person in less than 20 years indicates the practical usefulness of cell phones. The world simply works better with cell phones.

A number of unintended consequences, both proven and unproven, occur because of this technological advancement. For example, a number of automobile accidents involving other cars and pedestrians occur because drivers using cell phones are distracted and are less capable at the wheel. Other accidents occur when drivers drop their phone and then take their eyes off the road to search for the device. In addition, people have been robbed and even killed as muggers attempt to steal phones. But the mother-of-all unintended consequences from cell phone use may be a health risk potentially afflicting all users.

Cell phones arose from the Bell Labs, a research facility owned by the former telephone monopoly AT&T Corporation[248]. Cell phones work as a full duplex two-way radio transmitted over a series of connected cell sites. Basically the phones transmit and receive radio signals from cell sites. This flow of radio waves is measured as an amount of radiation and it has scientists concerned. The Federal Communications Commission regulates the amount of

---

[247] Randall Strauss, "Should You be Snuggling with Your Cell Phone?" *The New York Times*, November 15, 2010.

[248] Developments that came out of the Bell Labs include the transistor, the laser, and the UNIX operating system among others along with the thousands upon thousands of devices that have been created using these basic technologies.

radiation that can be absorbed by a cell phone user, a statistic referred to as the specific absorption rate (SAR). Some argue that SAR limits are too high. The most common health risk voiced regarding cell phones is the accusation that there is a positive relationship between the SAR level and cancer.

Research is currently not definitive on the question of whether cell phones induce human cancers. An epidemiologist, Devra Davis' book *Disconnect* has reawakened concerns about cell phone radiation.[249] She notes that while the overall incidence of brain cancer has not changed, the rate amongst high cell phone users, those aged 20 - 29, increased while the rate amongst the older population dropped.[250] Other studies, have found no relationship between cell phone use and cancer. The scientific debate is not over.

The stakes are very high; in the US wireless carriers generate over $109 billion in revenue. Professor Henry Lai found that of 400 scientific studies that he examined, when the wireless industry paid for or supported the research only 28% of the studies found any cancer effect but when studies were conducted without industries funding 67% of studies concluded that there was a relationship.[251] It will take a long time and a lot of money before we know definitively whether or not cell phone use is safe. In the meantime, health advocates suggest that children and young adults not be allowed to use cell phones (lots of luck with this) and that all users refrain from placing the phone besides their head and use beads or other technologies to reduce radiation absorption.

If the unintended consequences of cell phone use are limited to automobile accidents caused by texting or people wasting time on the job playing games on their smart phones, then the societal cost of cell phones is not too great. If, on the other hand, cell phones lead directly to cancer, then the

---

[249] Devra Davis, *Disconnect: The Truth About Cell Phone Radiation, What the Industry has Done to Hide it, How to Protect Your Family*, Dutton Adult, 2010.
[250] Stross, Op cit.
[251] Stross, Op cit.

unintended consequence of this technology are substantial, expensive, and ones that will cause the technology to change or else it may end cell phone use entirely.

How Social Media Creates Good and Bad

If you are my age, you might ask what social media is. Social media is social interaction on technological steroids. Social interaction is people getting together for a common purpose - such as when they hold a meeting. Unlike traditional media which includes TV, newspapers, radio, and film, social media is very inexpensive enabling individuals to have the power to reach out to others. Examples of social media include Twitter, Facebook, Wikipedia, blogs, and Yelp. A number of unintended consequences are associated with social media - some of which are good and some which are bad.

The rebellion against dictatorship referred to as the Arab Spring that began in December 2010 has led to revolutions in Tunisia, Egypt, Libya, Bahrain, Syria, amongst others. Most of these uprisings depended on the social media, notably YouTube, Facebook, and Twitter to organize and encourage sympathizers. The unintended consequence of the development of social media is that the individual now has the power to fight the efforts of the state to repress communications and organization amongst its opponents. The secret police with their mainframe computers and truncheons have proved powerless against the tapping thumbs of unhappy citizens.

Social media has also had undesirable unintended consequences. By using social media, criminals have generated flash mobs that descend upon retail establishments and rip them off. Riots in the UK in August 2011 spread via social media. There is little that several store clerks or individual police officers can do to restrain a dangerous mob set upon stealing or destruction. Technology such as video cameras has the potential to provide law enforcement with sufficient information to enable them to arrest the perpetrators of such acts. This negative unintended consequence has transformed shoplifting, which has been a problem since the first store opened, into a more threatening occurrence.

How Technology Changes Our Brains

Kids live in a different world today than they would have a few decades ago. It is rare to see someone between the ages of 12 and 30 walking down the street without an electronic device in their hands. Whether a cell phone, a small computer-pad for TV or movie viewing, or a videogame, kids are in constant communication with friends and the larger world. Older people don't understanding why anybody needs to know in real time what somebody else did this morning; or why somebody would send out a 1,000 texts a day. On the other hand, young people have skills their older peer's lack.

The unintended consequence of this barrage of electronic stimuli is the loss of other skills honed over millennia. Michael Rich a scientist at the Harvard medical school says, "Their brains are rewarded for not staying on task but for jumping to the next thing." [252] In some ways the human brain is like a large container; it only has room for so much stuff. Once it is filled it is hard to add more.

This is not the first generation of kids whose parents can't understand why they do certain things. In the 1960s, parents objected to rock and roll, sexual proclivity, and drug use. In the 1920s, it was jazz music, unchaperoned dating, and gin. There's always something that kids do that parents object to. What is worrisome about the unintended consequences caused by electronic devices is how they, by

---

[252] Matt Rictel, "Growing Up Digital, Wired for Distraction," *The New York Times*, November 21, 2010.

themselves, fill up the container in the brain and leave little room for anything else. Kids in the sixties who listened to rock and roll, experienced free love, and used marijuana still grew up to become doctors, lawyers, and fire chiefs. Those activities left room for young people to learn necessary skills. The fear today is that the younger generation will grow up good at texting and little else.

Psychologically the problem with texting and hyper communication about oneself is the failure to appreciate the larger world beyond the electronic fence of a texting device. Rather than learn skills that help a person to interact with others and to appreciate other things beyond one's self, textors seem to withdrawal into themselves or perhaps into a small circle of friends, with little regard for the rest of society. Jungian psychological theories might argue that this unintended consequence has unleashed an addictive and highly attractive technology that might lead to a form of introversion: self-absorption at the expense of everything else. [253] Although introversion has no pathological component, society may suffer if the normal mix of extroverts and introverts changes as the wave of technological sweeps across the globe.

Another aspect of this phenomenon is referred to as "transacted memory." [254] Transacted memory arises when a person thinks that someone else such as a coworker will remember a certain fact. When a person thinks that someone else will remember something they don't bother remembering it themselves e.g. maybe your gym locker if you always visit the gym with the same person or how many Super Bowls the Chicago Bears played in. Scientists have discovered that transacted memory extends to computers. [255]

---

[253] Jung, C.J. (1921). *Psychologischen Typen*, Rascher Verlag, Zurich – translation H.G. Baynes, 1923.

[254] Patricia Cohen, "Internet Use Affects How we Remember," *The New York Times*, July 15, 2011, A14.

[255] Sparrow, B., Liu, J., and Wegner, D. M. 2011, "Google Effects on Memory: Cognitive Consequences of Having Information at our Fingertips," *Science*, 10.1126/science.1207745.

People are better at remembering which folder on their computer contains information then in remembering the information itself. As long as the person has access to their computer or cloud storage area transacted memory does not impose too substantial an unintended consequence. But when the person's link to technology is broken as for example when they ride on an airplane the unintended consequence of not retaining information may be significant.

How Trying to Get Well Can Make Us Sick

Modern medicine is miraculous. Human life expectancy has increased from approximately 20 years during Neolithic times[256] to the current world wide average of 67 years. [257] A key element in expanding the length of a lifetime is the modern hospital. Hospitals perform organ transplant surgeries, cure some cancers, and enable 46% of heart attack patients who reach the hospital alive to survive. [258] The cost of building these healing centers has expanded too; for example, the Pennsylvania General Hospital was constructed in 1751 for £4,000 while the first phase of the new Cleveland Clinic in Abu Dhabi is expected to cost $1.9 billion.

Despite their technological and scientific wonders, modern hospitals pose an unintended consequence that kills many people each year. Errors occurring in hospitals, which are often controllable, lead to 98,000 deaths a year and more than 1 million injuries, in the US alone. [259] Over the six years

---

[256] Galor, Oded and Omer Moav, 2007, "The Neolithic Revolution and Contemporary Variations in Life Expectancy," *Brown University Working Paper*.

[257] CIA, *The World Factbook*, Rank Order - Life Expectancy at Birth.

[258] Cobbe SM, Dalziel K, Ford I, Marsden AK, June 1996, "Survival of 1476 patients initially resuscitated from out of hospital cardiac arrest". *BMJ* 312 (7047): 1633–7.

[259] Denise Grady, "Hospitals Make No Headway in Curbing Errors, Study Says," *The New York Times*, November 25, 2010.

2002 - 2007 approximately 25% of hospital admissions suffered some harm during their hospital stay. [260]

The three principle causes of hospital mistakes are human error, errors due to medical complexity, and systematic failures. [261] Human errors result from fatigue and there being insufficient time to treat patients; medical complexity errors include pharmacological interactions and unnecessary invasive tests; and systematic failures result from poor communications and the incorrect assumption that someone else is responsible. What causes hospital mistakes may also be responsible for hospital success. The forces that enable doctors and hospital system to extend human lives lead to unintended consequences that shorten life.

Obviously the solution is not to close down hospitals; rather, hospitals need to improve patient safety. Electronic record-keeping can help insure the delivery of proper pharmaceuticals in the right dosage. Unlike the airline industry whose industry-wide practices have led to near-perfect safety records and a clientele which expects a safe arrival, the medical profession confronts a basic biological inevitability that eventually all people must die. Consequently, doctors, hospitals, and patient families are not surprised when some patients succumb. That creates an environment more tolerant of errors.

It is hard to argue with the basic economic premise that people behave rationally. This means that people's behavior responds to incentives. For many people the best incentive is money though other incentives motivate people too. With sufficient financial incentives people will do most anything. That has led some advocates to suggest that the way to reduce the unintended consequence of hospital care errors is to move the medical profession to a pay-for-performance platform. A doctor or a hospital would be financially penalized if a patient succumbed to an avoidable error. Some argue that pay-for-performance breeds its own unintended

---

[260] Ibid.

[261] Weingart S.N., Wilson R.M., Gibberd R.W., Harrison B, March 2000, "Epidemiology of Medical Error," *BMJ*, 320 (7237): 774–7.

consequence: hospitals and physicians who avoid treating high-risk patients. [262] A number of experiments are in place seeking to demonstrate the efficacy of a pay for performance compensation system.

How Helmets May Be Worse Than No Helmet At All

It's Sunday afternoon and a legion of modern gladiators prepares to emerge from under the packed stands to do battle on the football field. Before leaving the dressing room these super athletes suit up wearing their team colors and protecting their bodies with the best technologies known to man including shoulder pads and protectors for their knees, kidneys, ankles, and elbows. Most crucial of all in the minds of players, coaches, and spectators is the helmet. Not only does the helmet present the team's emblem on either side of the player's head (except for the Cleveland Browns in the NFL) but with its inner padding, outer shell, and face bars it is thought to provide a high level of protection.

The earliest football helmets made of leather were introduced in the 1920s. Little more than protection against the weather, leather helmets were displaced by those made of plastic starting in the early 1940s. Since then a series of developments involving type of plastic, amount of inner padding, and the introduction of polycarbonate visors have turned helmets into a high-technology device. One would think that the number and severity of injuries would decline.

Concerns have recently been articulated about the health and well-being of current and retired football players. The principle focus of these concerns has been concussions. Concussions occur not from a brain bruise as is commonly believed but as a result of injury caused by rapid acceleration

---

[262] M .B. Rosenthal and R. G. Frank, 2006, "What Is the Empirical Basis for Paying for Quality in Health Care?" *Medical Care Research and Review* 63 (2): 135–57.

and then deceleration of the brain or from a violent spinning of the brain.[263] Medical science believes that concussions lead to physical and mental impairment including psychiatric problems, loss of memory, Parkinson's disease, and dementia pugilistica which is symptomatically similar to Alzheimer's.[264] The incidence of these ailments among retired football player exceeds levels found throughout the population.

There is a game played in Australia that is similar to football. Unlike American football, Australian players wear no body armor.[265] Australian players receive more injuries overall but American players suffer about 25% more head injuries.[266] This higher head injury rate may be an unintended consequence of protective headgear. Players wearing the full body armor of a modern football player and its heavy thick helmet develop a feeling of invincibility. As a result, many tackles are made using the head as a projectile rather than the shoulder or body. The unintended consequence of feeling indestructible may be that players injure their heads more frequently.

The myopia that allows an intelligent person to smoke cigarettes despite the overwhelming scientific evidence that cigarette smoking is harmful is likely to influence football player's behavior. With the threat of Parkinson's disease decades away and with football games played before adoring crowds in the present, it is unlikely that without league action that anything will reduce injuries on the football field. Individual players are fearful of being dropped from their team if they stop using their heads as projectiles. A similar problem is discussed in Chapter 2 regarding bicycles, "How Even Simple Governmental Restrictions have Consequences." The similarity concerns how motorcycle and bicycle riders

---

[263] "Head Injuries in Football," *The New York Times*, October 21, 2010.
[264] MF Mendez, 1995, "The Neuropsychiatric Aspects of Boxing". *International Journal of Psychiatry in Medicine* 25 (3): 249–62.
[265] Reed Albergotti and Shirley S Wang, "Is It Time to Retire the Football Helmet?" *The Wall Street Journal*, November 11, 2009.
[266] Ibid.

detest wearing helmets even though evidence strongly suggests that they should.

How Unwrinkled Clothing May Put a Wrinkle in Your Health

Back in the 1950s mothers spent hours each week in front of a mangle or attached to an ironing board in an effort to keep linen and clothing wrinkle free. Wrinkles arise when fibers in fabrics move after being jostled in a washing machine. [267] To combat the loss of creases and the presence of unsightly wrinkles, textile manufacturers infuse products with formaldehyde. Formaldehyde is an organic compound which in June 2011 the US National Toxicology Program described as being a known human carcinogen. Studies have found an association between formaldehyde exposure and the development of leukemia and nasopharyngeal cancer. Standards exist in various countries to limit human exposure to formaldehyde and for the present it appears that the greatest danger from formaldehyde exposure exists for workers, such as those in funeral parlors, rather than consumers.

Not having to iron fabric is one of the many laborsaving technologies that have radically altered family life. While it has not been as significant a laborsaving factor as refrigeration, microwave cooking, or vacuum cleaners, wrinkle-free fabrics have been a boon to modern existence. Whether or not exposure to formaldehyde on the skin of consumers from wrinkle-free materials will lead to greater health dangers than just dermatitis[268] only time will tell, but readers of this book will certainly realize that the possibility exists for greater danger in the future. Even after health

---

[267] Tara Siegel Bernard, "When Wrinkle Free Clothing Also Means Formaldehyde Fumes," *The New York Times*, December 11, 2010.
[268] Ibid.

warnings, embalmers are reluctant to change to a different technology.[269]

How The Wisdom of Crowds is Lost When We Know Too Much

James Surowiecki's compelling book argues that no single individual is as smart as the collective wisdom.[270] While there are situations where group behavior fails - as for example when markets overreact and create bubbles in housing or stocks- there are many examples where Surowiecki paradigm works. Two critical conditions are necessary for group think to be more accurate than individual thought are that people have multiple opinions and each person is autonomous and not influenced by others. Group thinking is very successful in predicting the outcome of political elections.

However, it is easy to disturb the delicate process wherein the "Crowd" is more intelligent than the individual. If individuals have access to the views of others, as they do with the Internet, then the accuracy of group thinking declines.[271] People change their opinions when they know that others have a different view; that is an unintended consequence of knowing too much. Economic forecasting has long suffered from this problem. Economic forecasters are a close knit group who meet together and converse on a regular basis. When economic forecast are examined most of them fall into a tight range and as a result when one misses

---

[269] Andrew Martin, "Despite Risk, Embalmers Still Embrace Preservative," *The New York Times*, July 20, 2011.
[270] James Surowiecki, *The Wisdom of Crowds: Why the Many are Smarter Than the Few and How Collective Wisdom Shapes Business, Economies, Societies and Nations*, 2004, Doubleday, 2004.
[271] Jonah Lehrer, "When We're Cowed by the Crowd," The *Wall Street Journal*, May 28, 2011.

an economic turning point (i.e., a recession or recovery) they all tend to miss it. Since society will not reduce the dissemination of news and information it is prudent to advise people to be careful of the unintended consequence caused by a crowd that knows too much.

How Biologists Must Not Have Been on Noah's Ark

At one time biologist thought they could perfect their environment by manipulating the diversity of life in particular locations. Nature has a way of making things perfect. Sometimes this perfection irritates people who must swat away mosquitoes or learn to tolerate unbearable humidity. When people think they are smarter than nature is when unintended consequences emerge. Several examples highlight this.

China has suffered from famine throughout much of its long history; the disruption to the nation's agriculture during the long communist uprising led by Mao Zedong (1927 – 1949) made matters worse. Thinking that he had a better understanding of nature, Mao ordered the Chinese people to kill the four "pests:" flies, insects, rats, and sparrows. He believed that food production would increase without these creatures. His plan may have worked had it not been for unintended consequences. Without predators controlling them the number of locusts and grasshoppers multiplied and they devoured tons of food resulting in mass starvation.

The cane toad is another example of how scientists misapplied their knowledge and changed nature only to be hit by an unintended consequence. [272] Cane toads are poisonous with a voracious appetite. These killing machines were thought to be a simple pest control system. The cane toad was introduced in various locations (Australia, the US, New

---

[272] Mark Gongloff, "To Be Learned: Bear Stearns Consequences," *The Wall Street Journal,* April 7, 2008.

Guinea, the Caribbean, and Fiji) at various times mostly in the 1930s. The unintended consequence was that the toads were too successful and soon overran the regions altering the biodiversity and upsetting the natural balance.

How Having More Information May Actually be Less

A fascinating article by James Evans of the University of Chicago uncovered an amazing unintended consequence.[273] He analyzed the impact of academic journals being available in digital format. One argument for the digitization of academic articles is that it allows them to be more widely distributed. Evidence of broader dissemination, one would expect, would be that more journal articles received citations from other scholars. Professor Evans obtained data on the citation rate for 34 million academic articles published over the period 1945 - 2005. One would expect that as the Internet became more pervasive, and articles became digitize, that there would be less concentration in the citation record of journal articles. His results did not confirm this.

Professor Evans notes that academics make wide use of Internet search engines. A search for a broad topic like corporate bankruptcy might return over 100,000 links. Obviously, no one actually views all available links. Search engines rank academic articles according to their citation count. Putting these two facts together - search engines return massive amounts of data and the most cited articles appear at the top of the search - causes fewer articles to actually be cited now that technology is available. This unintended consequence has important significances for young researchers whose work is not published in the very top journals. It has and will become increasingly difficult for

---

[273] James Evans, "Electronic Journals and the Narrowing of Science and Scholarship," *Science,* 321: 395-399. 2008.

academic work not precisely conforming to mainstream theories to gain a foothold amongst peers.

If technology has made it more difficult for new research to gain recognition (via peer citations) then science will become stultified and less creative. This is an unintended consequence for which there are few if any remedies. It is unlikely that any university will restrict access to search engines by its researchers or will demand that they review all search results before writing it up.

Chapter 6

Corporate Unintended Consequences

How Rules Rule

The cost of providing medical care may soon bankrupt this country. Sit down before reading about data available in the National Health Expenditure Accounts. In 1960 the US spent $27.5 billion ($148 per capita) on health expenditures an amount representing 5.2% of GDP; by 2008 that amount had risen to $2.3 trillion ($7,681 per capita) or 16.2% of GDP. [274] This spending level and rate of growth are terrifying. On the other hand, these dollars helped increase

---

[274] US Department of Health and Human Services, Centers for Medicare and Medicaid Services, National Health Expenditure Data, 2008.

the average life span from 70 years in 1960 to 78.4 years in 2008.[275] Any civilization would be imperiled if it devoted so many resources to this end. Ancient Egypt's ultimate demise is attributed to that society's application of much of its national resources to the dead through the construction of pyramids and the preparation of mummies.

The unintended consequence in this section concerns primary care physicians (PCP). The PCP is the doctor that most patients contact when they initially need care. Some insurance plans position the PCP as a gatekeeper who decides whether a patient should see a more costly specialist. Despite the critical position of PCPs in the medical hierarchy there is a shortage of PCPs. In the US, between 1997 and 2005 the number of medical students training for family practice dropped by 50%.[276] Arguably this occurred because of the way doctors get paid.

Starting in 1992 Medicare created a paradigm called the resource based relative value system (RBRVS) to evaluate doctors. Since then, insurance companies have used RBRVS as a means to determine compensation for doctors. That work is assisted by the Specialty Society Relative Value Scale Update Committee (RUC). RUC assesses a doctor's training and work effort. Greater detail on RUC is provided in Chapter 7's section entitled How the Medical Gate Keeper is like a Lighthouse Keeper. Basically the methodology bifurcates medical activities into those that involve procedures and those that don't. Doctors who perform procedures such as surgeons are well compensated; in contrast, PCPs whose work is more analytical than procedural are less well compensated. The signal given by relative compensations of various specialties creates a powerful unintended consequence.

---

[275] World Bank, *World Development Indicators*, October 22, 2010.
[276] American Academy of Family Physicians, National Resident Matching Program Data: Family Medicine Residency Positions and Number Filled by US Medical School Graduates, 1994-2006.

People are rational. If you offer kids the possibility of earning millions playing basketball rather than studying mathematics or science, kids acquire basketball skills. Likewise, a young medical student anticipating graduating from medical school with a $350,000 debt load responds to compensation signals rationally and shuns primary care medicine in favor of fields that involve procedures and higher compensation.

This unintended consequence derives from insurance companies deciding to support a non-market based compensation rule. This decision is ill founded because in most situations markets work. For example, an inferior restaurant will fail if it tries to charge similar prices as does a restaurant which serves better food; consumers pick the restaurant providing the most quality for their money. A compensation rule for medical professionals that distorts market signals leads to an inappropriate mix of doctors. The misallocation of doctors creates a societal cost problem for several reasons.

First, the PCP is the point man in the medical profession. His/her role as a diagnostician who administers advice, medicine, and permission to see other doctors is vital to the functioning of the entire system. Worse, it is difficult for a person to get a PCP. There simply aren't enough of them to go around. Secondly, artificially populating the medical profession with too many specialists, who know how to perform complex and expensive procedures, results in too many procedures being performed. Under the current system, since more of the work effort is performed by the highest paid among the profession the total cost of medical care to society rises.

An entire chapter, Chapter 7, is devoted to the medical industry. This discussion appears in the corporate chapter though it could equally have been part of Chapter 7.

How Fear Leads to Inaction

Possibly the most annoying thing about the Internet is that surfing activities are being observed and recorded by marketing companies. These companies profit by directing advertisers to likely buyers based on their previous search behavior. The idea is elegant in its simplicity: send an advertisement for an online shoe vendor to someone who's looking to buy a new pair of shoes. In theory at least the buyer and the shoe vendor are happy with this arrangement. Privacy advocates don't agree. They object to the idea of anyone snooping on personal Internet activities; their concern has less to do with the commercial aspect of snooping and more to do with the fact that every keystroke, page view, and search request is observed by a third party who has not asked permission to do so.

Internet users are not alone and defenseless in this battle. Their big allies in the battle with these snoops are the browser developers: Firefox, Safari, and Explorer. At the end of the summer of 2010, Mozilla Corp., the developer of the Firefox browser, reportedly removed a tool that could have limited online tracking.[277] Suspicion was that Mozilla had been pressured by the advertising industry to make the change. But that is not what happened.

Instead, Mozilla reports that it considered what would likely happen if they included the anti-tracking tool in the new version of Firefox. In their view, there would likely be an unintended consequence; advertisers would develop new more pernicious methods of snooping.[278] If this were to happen websites across the Internet might not be as easy to download. Because of the fear of this unintended consequence, Mozilla decided to not include the new anti-

---

[277] Julia Angwin and Spencer E. Ante, "Hiding Online Footprints," *The Wall Street Journal*, November 30, 2010.
[278] Ibid.

snooping tool. This is a rare example of a company that reviewed its actions for unintended consequences <u>before</u> making a decision.[279]

It seems that the extent of snooping is going to do nothing but get worse. Advertisers are interested in being able to send highly targeted messages. In order to do that companies are now developing the means to identify specific electronic devices based on a unique digital fingerprint. [280] One company, BlueCava Inc., has already identified 200 million out of the world's 10 billion electronic devices. In the same way that swirls in fingerprints distinguish between people, electronic devices can be distinguished by which fonts are uploaded onto the device, the sequence of when the fonts were uploaded, and many other seemingly innocuous features that differentiate one device from the next. This may elevate snooping to a whole new level.

How Greed Leads to Bad Decision-Making

Large automobile companies sell to many different customer types including new families with young children, young singles, retired people, and working couples. The vehicle needs of each group differ: a young family is looking for a way to transport children and their gear, a young single person wants a flashy small car, retired people are looking for inexpensive transportation, and working couples have a variety of needs. Product mix diversity creates problems by requiring manufacturers to supply a variety of vehicles

---

[279] On December 8, 2010 Microsoft Corporation reported that its new Internet Explorer 9 would contain a tracking protection list that users could enable and thereby avoid having their Internet browsing monitored by advertising companies.

[280] Julia Angwin and Jennifer Valentino-Devries, "Race is on to Fingerprint Phones, PCs," *The Wall Street Journal*, December 1, 2010.

(product platforms and other techniques reduce the multi-product penalty). On the other hand, a diversified product mix protects manufacturers against the vagaries of consumer demand.

The sport utility vehicle (SUV) was practically unheard of until the early 1990s when Chrysler popularized the product type. [281] Ford and General Motors were not far behind. At first the SUV had advantages for both the manufacturer and the customers. Manufacturers benefited because unlike cars which were subject to the corporate average fuel economy standard (CAFE), SUVs were sold as work vehicles, i.e., trucks. SUVs were not required to comply with CAFE and automobile companies did not have to invest to raise their average fuel economy. More importantly, the profit margin on an SUV might be $20,000 while for cars it rarely exceeded $1,000. Consumers benefited because SUVs provided larger interior space and a higher riding platform; they also gave the perception of being safer than cars though evidence on this conjecture is mixed.

American automobile manufacturers ceded the small car market to foreign producers and concentrated on SUVs. The lower wage structure of foreign producers, many of whom were not unionized by the UAW, contributed to the American abandonment of the small automobile market. Another reason for the emphasis on SUVs was that American manufacturers had a head start over their foreign competition. Though a similar dominance had been true in the automobile sector, over time new companies had caught up and surpassed American vehicles based on quality, efficiency, and functionality. Very little effort was given during the late 1990s and early 2000 by American car companies to improving and enhancing their automotive products.

---

[281] Early SUVs such as the Chevrolet Carryall Suburban, introduced in 1935, were not big sellers and were rarely seen.

The unintended consequence of this corporate decision hit when oil prices spiked upwards. In early 2004 oil was selling for $40 a barrel. It reached a peak of nearly $140 a barrel in early 2008. All of a sudden consumers were willing to forgo the luxury and ease of a large SUV in favor of smaller fuel-efficient vehicles. American car companies were unable to deliver the vehicle types that consumers wanted because they had effectively abandoned this portion of the market. The bankruptcy of General Motors and Chrysler in 2009 resulted from both the unintended consequence of their pursuing a narrow yet profitable market segment as well as the near total collapse of the American economy during the subprime mortgage debacle. Within a few short years American car manufacturers went from their most profitable years ever to bankruptcy.

How Success Leads to Bad Decision-Making

After trouncing American car companies by offering high-quality precision engineered vehicles such as the Camry, Corolla, and various Lexus models, Toyota Motor Corporation decided to pursue a strategy of market domination. The plan was to roll out a succession of attractive vehicles targeting virtually every segment of the American automobile market. In order to do that, Toyota needed to develop, design, source, and manufacture a large number of new vehicles in a short period of time. The plan was to overwhelm the Big Three automakers. But as they say, there is a long way between the cup and the lip.

It's not easy to develop new vehicles at least if you wante to produce cars that match the high quality standards of Toyota. The unintended consequence of the pursuit of this new strategy was that between November 2009 and early 2010 Toyota recalled approximately 8 million vehicles. Some of the recalled vehicles reportedly had safety issues such as accelerators that stuck, others had mechanical problems. At one point they even halted production and sales of several cars. Toyota's market share in America has risen every year since the brand was introduced in the mid-1960s. In 2009 market share reached 16.7%.[282] Following the automobile recall announcements, 2010 was the first year in which Toyota's market share declined. (Honda's market share also fell in 2010 but by less than Toyotas.[283])

Propelling Toyota onward was a long string of successes. It must have seemed to executives that every new product they introduced would be accepted to glowing praises by the consuming public. Quality was never dropped from the Toyota equation but management failed to understand that there are practical limits to growth. Whether Toyota can recover from the unintended consequence of trying to sell lower quality vehicles to a public which had come to expect only the best from it is hard to predict. But the lessons learned should guide other companies embarking on a new strategy to consider potential unintended consequences.

How Beauty is not in the Eye of the Beholder

Anorexia nervosa (AN) is a severe eating disorder. Victims of AN perceive themselves to have excessive body weight and they obsessively seek to lose weight. While some victims die from starvation and many survivors suffer from it for years, the vast majority of AN sufferers get well.[284]

---

[282] Mike Ramsey and Chester Dawson, "Toyota, Honda Lose US Edge," *The Wall Street Journal*, November 15, 2010.
[283] Ibid.
[284] J I Hudson, E Hiripi, Harlan G Pope, RC Kessler, 2007, "The Prevalence and Correlates of Eating Disorders in the National

In a historical context anorexia nervosa is a relatively new malady. Reports from the 1800s of "fasting girls" who deprived their bodies of nourishment for religious reasons are thought by some to be early references to AN. [285] Since then modern medicine has worked hard to better understand the disease. We now know that 10 times as many women as men are afflicted with AN, that many sufferers purge to voluntarily excise calories from their bodies, and that most undergo severe physical changes such as swollen cheeks, rapid weight loss, and hirsuitism, the growth of fine hairs over most of their face and body. [286] AN afflicts 1% of all women and 0.1% of all men.[287] While the precise causes of AN are uncertain some medical scientist believe that weight loss caused by dieting may precipitate it while others suggest a hereditary predisposition. [288]

In contrast to medical observations about the causes of AN, there may be a cultural responsibility for the disease. I refer to the intense focus our society and media place on a person's physical appearance. Celebrity is no longer derived solely from accomplishment but now includes or highlights how one looks or misbehaves. The body shape that permeates much of this attention is one of extreme leanness. Fashion magazines rarely if ever present models whose body shapes resemble those of normal people, store windows are populated by manikins with ultra slim body builds, and TV shows and movies cast parts for the beautiful and chic

---

Comorbidity Survey Replication," *Biological Psychiatry* 61 (3): 348–58, February.

[285] Joan Jacobs Brumberg, *Fasting Girls: The History of Anorexia Nervosa*, 2000.

[286] JM Walsh, ME Wheat, K Freund, 2000, "Detection, Evaluation, and Treatment of Eating Disorders the Role of the Primary Care Physician". *Journal of General Internal Medicine* 15 (8): 577–90. August.

[287] J Treasure, AM Claudino, N Zucker, 2010, "Eating Disorders," *Lancet* 375 (9714): 583–93 February.

[288] BM Brandenburg, AE Andersen, 2007, "Unintentional Onset of Anorexia Nervosa, " *Eating and Weight Disorders* 12 (2): 97–100. June.

characters with slim almost abnormal body shapes. For a time, until preempted by a public outcry, fashionable appearance was defined as "heroin chic" because heroin users experience changes in their body shapes for much the same reason, limited caloric intake, as affects AN patients. Fashion models during the heroin chic phase were so slim as to seem breakable in a stiff wind. News articles of fashion models dying from AN are not infrequent.

Adolescents and preadolescence are bombarded daily by hundreds or thousands of images of ultrathin beauties. With both parents in many families working, there is often insufficient parental control over what youngsters watch and read. While not every adolescent compares their normal body to the AN starved look and concludes that they are overweight, in some cases the unintended consequence of how beauty is portrayed in our society is that some young people decide that they are overweight. Dieting has become something that almost everybody does all the time. Some dieters trying to look more "model-like" may initiate the medical conditions associated dieting with AN. Whatever the precise cause of this plague it is hard to deny the culpability of corporations who indifferently present extreme visions of beauty to young susceptible adolescents. Companies need to control themselves and stop engaging in practices with known unintended consequences that harm the very young and unprotected.

How Cigarette Smokers Hurt Those Near Them

Cigarette smoking is an addictive habit. Though nicotine acetylcholine is not itself addictive its impact on dopamine-releasing neurons leads to addiction and is similar to the effect of cocaine on the human body.[289] You know a product is highly addictive when a large percentage of its users admit that they would like to stop but cannot. As a former smoker I can tell you that the craving did not go away entirely for seven years.

People start smoking for a variety of reasons; to look cool, because everyone around them is smoking, and because they believe that smoking calms their nerves, keeps them thin, or makes food taste better. After the addiction takes hold people smoke because they have to. One reason smoking leads to many health-related problems is because addictiveness makes it a long-term habit. Few people smoke for just a short time.

Although no addiction (including drugs, food, liquor, or sex) affects just the doer, smoking has a particularly onerous unintended consequence upon those near to the smoker. It is often labeled as "secondhand smoke." Scientific evidence suggests that second-hand smoke is responsible for the same illnesses - cardiovascular disease, various cancers, and respiratory ailments -as primary smoking.[290] A recent study has found that secondhand smoke leads to hearing loss.[291] What makes these secondhand illnesses so unfortunate is that the victims received none of the perceived benefits of smoking. Instead, whether they are a bartender, an airline steward (believe it or not people used to smoke on airplanes), or the spouse or child of a smoker, their health is permanently damaged by the smoker's addiction.

---

[289] F. E Pontieri, G Tanda, F Orzi, and G. D Chiara, 1996, "Effects of Nicotine on the Nucleus Accumbens and Similarity to those of Addictive Drugs," *Nature* 382 (6588): 255.
[290] Surgeon General of the United States, 2006, *The Health Consequences of Involuntary Exposure to Tobacco Smoke: A Report of the Surgeon General*, June, 27.
[291] Jeremy Singer-Vine, "Secondhand Smoke may Harm Non-Smokers Hearing," *The Wall Street Journal*, November 30, 2010.

More recently, a new variation on this unintended consequence has emerged that is called "third-hand smoke." Third-hand smoke refers to tobacco smoke contaminants that linger on surfaces after secondhand smoke has dissipated. [292] As a result of this unintended consequence, unsuspecting parents may harm their infant children by allowing them to crawl in a room formerly occupied by smokers, pets are harmed when they simply roll around in the home of a smoker, and anyone visiting a smoker's home may be subjected to later health problems. Oddly, tobacco warnings on cigarette packs focus solely on the health of the smoker. Perhaps graphic pictures of sick children or pets might do more to control this unintended consequence than warnings given to addicted individuals.

How Fishing for Solutions Smells Fishy

Growing world population and rising income levels has led to overfishing in many parts of the world. As much as 70% of fish species are below sustainable levels as a consequence of commercial overfishing.[293] One solution to this problem is fish farming. As its name suggests fish are raised and harvested outside of their natural habitat. The business accounts for as much as 50% of the world's fish production[294]. Some farmed fish crops like bivalves are actually good for the ecosystem since oysters and mussels eat waste products in the water. Others crops such as farm raised salmon have the environmentally unfriendly requirement of needing three or four pounds of smaller fish

---

[292] GE Matt, PJ Quintana, MF Hovell, *et al.*, 2004, "Households Contaminated by Environmental Tobacco Smoke: Sources of Infant Exposures," *Tobacco Control* 13 (1): 29–37, March.
[293] Travis Walter Donovan, "Nine Surprising Fish Farming Facts," *Huffington Post*, May 31, 2010.
[294] "Fish Farming," foodreference.com, accessed December 7, 2010.

to be harvested and processed to yield a single pound of product.

Fish farming has a number of negative unintended consequences. Among these are the fouling of nearby waters through the discharge of waste products and antibiotics administered to keep the fish healthy, breeding issues caused by escaped farmed fish, chemically laced fish products imported from overseas farms, and the destruction of natural habitats to make room for fish farms. Certain countries have carefully controlled the industry to minimize negative consequences and to improve the quality of the output. In those cases, negative unintended consequences are kept as low as possible.

Recently a surprising negative unintended consequence of fish farming arose in the Great Lakes area. The problem originated in the 1970s from the decision of fish farmers in the Mississippi Delta to import Asian carp whose task was to clean fish pens (by eating the waste) housing farmed fish. [295] The idea on its surface made sense; carp have been farm raised in China for centuries, they are bottom fish who eat other fishes' waste, and there is a ready market for carp. Sometimes the surface isn't deep enough. Lurking below the surface are several unfortunate facts: bighead carp weigh as much as 100 pounds, silver carp leap 10 feet out of the water and accidentally injure boat passengers, both varieties reproduce rapidly and all varieties of carp are ravenous eaters. During the 1990s when the Mississippi Delta flooded the carp escaped from fish farms. [296] Since then they have made their way up the Mississippi River in an unrelenting gluttonous feast on their way to the Great Lakes. Along the way they have devoured the normal food stock of native species (they do not eat other fish) causing those fishes to either starve or relocate.

---

[295] Douglas Belkin, "States Cast for Way to Stop the Carp," *The Wall Street Journal*, December 4, 2009.
[296] Ibid.

Recreational fishing in the Great Lakes produces $7 billion annually for local economies.[297] Should the migrating carp reach the Great Lakes, an economic disaster might ensue. Unlike fish native to the Great Lakes, carp flesh is laced with intricate bone structures making for unpleasant eating experiences and hence a lack of interest by recreational fishermen. Electric fences and poisonous solutions have so far kept carp out of the lakes but the prognosis is not good and the negative unintended consequences are expected to harm the area.

Like so many unintended consequences, probably because they arise unexpectedly, the Asian carp has rapidly entered the parlance of American culture. For example, a front-page *The New York Times* article on December 9, 2010 on the topic of romance novels includes the following reference to them, "the romance reader is a little like the Asian carp: insatiable and unstoppable."[298]

How Someone is Not Always Responsible

A terrible tragedy happened in July 2000 at the Charles de Gaulle airport outside Paris when a Concorde jet belonging to Air France crashed immediately after takeoff. Evidence gathered at the scene suggested that a piece of metal which fell off of a Continental Airline plane immediately before the accident had been thrown by the Concorde's tires into the jet's engines causing a fire and the crash which killed 113 people. Tragedies such as this one are rare occurrences in the aviation field and normally end after a safety commission determines the cause of the accident so that further incidents do not occur.

---

[297] Ibid.
[298] Julie Bosman, "Lusty Tales and Hot Sales: Romance Novels Thrive as E-Books," *The New York Times*, December 9, 2010.

That's not quite how the situation went in the case of the crash of the Concorde. Continental Airlines was accused by the French government of involuntary homicide in the deaths of the 109 people on the plane and four more on the ground. In December 2010 a French court ruled against Continental Airlines and forced it to pay fines and damages. Air France's lawyer said that the case had "national interests" suggesting that it was important to finger a foreigner as being responsible for the tragedy. [299] While there may be some truth to the notion of protecting a national interest, the verdict had the additional result of criminalizing an accident.

The aviation field has experienced an unprecedented reduction in the number of accidents over the past 40 years. While it is true that at one point air travel was hazardous, because of the efforts of thousands of people air travel is practically the safest form of travel in the world. Data suggests that the worldwide (US carriers are substantially safer than most others) risk (calculated as deaths per billion passenger's kilometers) of air travel is 62 times lower than for automobiles and 2,200 times lower than for motorcycles. In other words, air travel is amazingly safe. The unintended consequence is that a verdict criminalizing this accident may create reasons for companies, their employees, and other parties to stop cooperating with governmental investigators into the causes of future accidents. If that were to happen then future progress in making air travel safer would come to an end. That would be a tragedy.

How Subsidizing An Industry can Harm the World

In a move reminiscent of the government's damaging the housing market (see Chapter 2, How Government

---

[299] Daniel Michaels and Andy Pasztor, "Heated Safety Debate Follows Concord Verdict," *The New York Times*, December 7, 2010.

Encourage the 2007 Housing Bust) Washington subsidized the production of ethanol from corn as a partial replacement for gasoline. This section is not in the chapter on governmental unintended consequences because the lobbying effort and the push for additional subsidies came from farmers and other business people.

Corn, or maize, is the most widely grown grain in the US yielding over 330 million metric tons annually. 40% of this crop is used to make fuel for automobiles with barely half that amount devoted to human consumption. It is the fuel use that represents the unintended consequence. The idea is not new; Henry Ford's first car was designed to run on ethanol and his Model T could use gasoline or ethanol.[300] In 2001, the US produced 1,770 million liquid gallons of ethanol; by 2010 this number had increased to 13,230, quite a jump for a little yellow kernel. The increase in ethanol consumption was not driven by the marketplace; instead government subsidies and mandates drove the expansion. In 2005 and 2007 federal legislation required refineries to use a mixture of ethanol in gasoline.[301] This benefited corn farmers. To mollify any concerns amongst refiners, they were given a $0.45 a gallon subsidy to mitigate any cost differentials.

The score card comparing ethanol to gasoline comes out in gasoline's favor when the unintended consequences of ethanol fuels are included. To start with the scientific element, a gallon of ethanol yields only two-thirds the energy content of a gallon of gasoline and automobiles have lower miles per gallon with mixed fuels than pure gasoline. The production of a unit of ethanol requires the expenditure of

---

[300] J. Goettemoeller, A. Goettemoeller, 2007, *Sustainable Ethanol: Biofuels, Biorefineries, Cellulosic Biomass, Flex-Fuel Vehicles, and Sustainable Farming for Energy Independence*, Prairie Oak Publishing, Maryville, Missouri. p.42.
[301] Steven Rattner, "The Great Corn Con," *The New York Times*, June 25, 2011.

75% as much fossil fuel energy; little energy is gained in the exchange. Moreover, ethanol produces more carbon dioxide than does an equivalent energy amount of gasoline. Finally, it is more difficult to start automobiles in cold weather when gasoline has been mixed with ethanol.

The unintended consequence of ethanol use begins with its impact on farmland. By inducing farmers to produce more corn other crops are not produced. Consumers pay higher prices for those other crops; this cost increase might have been offset by lower corn prices but corn prices have instead reached record highs. Higher corn prices lead to price inflation at US grocery stores for consumers of soft drinks and other food items sweetened with corn syrup. The problem of food price inflation is particularly acute in less developed regions where income levels are low and achieving the subsistence caloric intake becomes difficult after the increase in corn prices.

A second unintended consequence is that other possibly more suitable crops such as sugarcane are not being adequately used to create an alternative to gasoline. Sugar cane for example, only requires 55% (rather than 75% for ethanol) as much fossil fuel energy to be produced. Sugarcane also has a smaller carbon footprint than either ethanol or gasoline.

Finally, in a perverse unintended consequence, the subsidy given to refiners makes ethanol cheaper to produce than gasoline. As a result, the US exports ethanol fuel while it simultaneously imports crude oil. [302] The logic of such a transaction is unfathomable.

---

[302] Ibid.

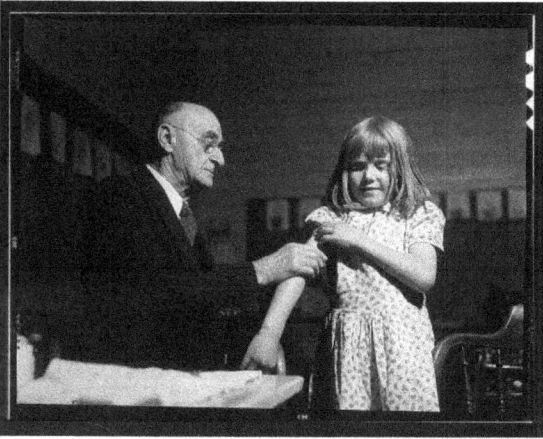

Chapter 7

Medical Unintended Consequences

Previous chapters have focused on broad topics such as technology rather than on specific areas such as medical care. Tip O'Neill said, "All politics is local." With unintended consequences while the parallel statement "all unintended consequences concern medicine" is untrue, it is true the most important thing to each of us is our health and that depends on medicine. However, the cost of medical care will soon bankrupt all governments - federal state and local. This book is not the forum to solve the medical conundrum; instead, it highlights the medical care problem in so far as they create unintended consequences.

Let's start out by defining the size of the problem. Medical care in the US accounted for approximately 16% of

GDP in 2009.[303] By the end of this decade, over 20% of GDP is expected to go to medical care.[304] Despite this extraordinary expenditure it is estimated that over 50 million residents (about 40 million citizens) are uninsured. Moreover, US life expectancy ranks just 42nd in the world despite our medical care having the highest cost.[305] Governments pay about 45% of all health care expenditures with remaining funds coming from employer-provided insurance, private insurance, and co-pays. [306]

As mentioned earlier, the Pharaohs bankrupted Egypt by building edifices to house the dead. While nothing similar is happening in the US, studies show that expenditures for those approaching the end of their life constitute a disproportionately large share of overall health care costs (remember the death panel debate).[307] Other studies have shown vast regional variation in the use of and expenditure on intensive healthcare for those near death. [308] The same studies do not report similar variations in life

---

[303] WHO, May 2009, *World Health Statistics 2009*, World Health Organization.

[304] Sean Keehan, Andrea Sisko, Christopher Truffer, Sheila Smith, Cathy Cowan, John Poisal, M. Kent Clemens, and the National Health Expenditure Accounts Projections Team, "Health Spending Projections Through 2017: The Baby-Boom Generation Is Coming To Medicare", *Health Affairs* Web Exclusive, February 26, 2008.

[305] United Nations World Population Prospects: 2006 revision -Table A.17 United Nations Department of Economic and Social Affairs, *World Population Prospects: The 2006 Revision*.

[306] CMS Annual Statistics, United States Department of Health and Human Services.

[307] Center for Health Workforce Studies, "The Impact of the Aging Population on the Health Workforce in the United States: Summary of Key Findings, March 2006.

[308] John E. Wennberg, Elliott S. Fisher, David C. Goodman, and Jonathan S. Skinner, "Tracking the Care of Patients with Severe Chronic Illness: the Dartmouth Atlas of Health Care 2008." The Dartmouth Institute for Health Policy and Clinical Practice, May 2008.

expectancy. One conclusion is that dollars alone are not a solution for the medical care system.

How Forgetting What Comes First Leads to Chaos

The story about the chicken and the egg refers to the problem of what comes first. Arguments can be made for both the chicken and the egg. An egg cannot be produced unless you have chickens but chickens cannot be born without an egg. The same dilemma applies to medical care. In order to control the overall cost of medical care, efforts have sought to shrink the cost of medical training. But without an adequate number of well-trained doctors, medical care costs rise.

In 1996, Congress passed legislation that limited the number of new doctors Medicare would pay to train. Medicare funds cover about 2/3rds of the cost of medical training. [309] More recently, President Obama's National Commission on Fiscal Responsibility and Reform, proposed further cuts in this budget. For a President whose signature legislation, the Patient Protection and Affordable Care Act of 2010 - otherwise known as Obamacare -will add 32 million newly insured individuals into the healthcare system, how they are to be cared for without new doctors is a mystery. [310] To accommodate just these new patients the number of doctors in the US must increase by 20%. In addition, more doctors are required to replace the 30% of current doctors intending to retire within the next decade. [311]

---

[309] Herbert Pardes, "The Coming Doctor Shortage," *The Wall Street Journal*, January 19, 2011.
[310] Ibid.
[311] Ibid.

Nearly 1/3rd of all hospitals are losing money. Budgetary issues are especially difficult for teaching hospitals. Without government funding it is uncertain who will pay to train new doctors. The unintended consequence of governmental limitations on funding medical training for young doctors coming at the same time as governmental regulations promising the delivery of medical care to tens of millions of people is that there will not be enough doctors for all. It is already difficult to get a doctor in many regions of the country; it will only get worse. Instead of a system where medical care is allocated to those with enough money to buy insurance or to pay for medical care on their own without insurance, the unintended consequence of these governmental policies is that we are moving to a system where medical care will be rationed or unavailable.

How Lawsuits Lead to Needless Medical Procedures

Hospitals, doctors, pharmaceutical companies, and everyone else associated with medical care in the US is terrified of medical malpractice lawsuits. Out of a population of 312 million people, in 2010, just 9,894 medical malpractice lawsuits received any payment. [312] In total these claims collected $3,328,708,700 or $336,437 per claim. These aggregate figures exclude the cost of lawyers, representing plaintiffs and defendants, the cost of unnecessary medical care provided in order to avoid possible lawsuits and the cost to patients who failed to find a physician willing to undertake a risky procedure in a challenging medical case.

While fewer than 10,000 medical malpractice cases receive payments in any year, many more cases are actually

---

[312] Statehealthfacts.org, Kaiser family foundation, extracted August, 9, 2011.

filed. It is estimated that 60% of medical malpractice lawsuits result in payments to the plaintiff with an associated legal cost of defending these case averaging over $22,000. [313] In the remaining 40% of cases, doctors were exonerated 90% of the time, after spending an average of $110,000 in defense costs. [314] Legal fees incurred by plaintiffs or their lawyers are not included in these cost estimates.

The unintended consequence of the proliferation of medical malpractice lawsuits is the advent of defensive medicine which includes unnecessary diagnostic testing, hospital stays, and prescriptions aimed at preparing a defense if a future loss suit should be filed. A study by Price Waterhouse Coopers LLP, prepared for the insurer's group America's Health Insurance Plans, in 2006 suggested that 10% of medical cost were absorbed by "malpractice lawsuits and more intensive diagnostic testing due to defensive medicine." [315] Health spending in the US is estimated to be $2.3 trillion according to Amitabh Chandra an economist at Harvard University. [316] Combining his estimate with Price Waterhouse Cooper's number suggests that the annual cost of this unintended consequence may be nearly $230 billion. The practice of defensive medicine is especially common in risky medical fields such as emergency care and obstetrics which experience a disproportionate number of medical malpractice-lawsuits. Some analysts estimate that the cost of defensive medicine runs as high as 93% in high-risk medical fields. [317] Dollar estimates are unavailable for patient cost arising from unnecessary stress, needless medical testing, and time away from family.

---

[313] *The Case for Medical Liability Reform*", American Medical Association, November 2009.
[314] Ibid.
[315] Alex Nussbaum, *Bloomberg*, "Malpractice Lawsuits are Red Herring in Obama Plan," June 16, 2009.
[316] Ibid.
[317] http://jama.ama-assn.org/cgi/content/abstract/293/21/2609.

A second unintended consequence arising from medical malpractice claims is that doctors in training avoid studying high risk fields. Moreover, older doctors not yet at retirement age retire once the cost of medical malpractice insurance consumes too large a share of their gross income. Both affects reduce the number of doctors available to perform needed yet risky medical procedures.

How the Bright Lights of Big Cities Hurts the Country

There are 133 medical schools in the US with an additional 28 granting a doctor of osteopathic medicine degree. The vast majority of these institutions are located in large cities which have a teaching hospital with thousands of attendant personnel and patients. A small number of these schools are located in smaller cities such as East Tennessee State University in Johnson City Tennessee or the University of South Dakota in Sioux Falls South Dakota. Regardless of where they go to medical school, most medical school graduates are attracted to the bright lights and higher salary levels of big cities.

Arguably there are not enough doctors overall in the US. An unintended consequence of medical school's location and higher salaries paid doctors in urban areas has made the supply-of-doctors problem more critical in certain areas. There is an imbalance in the distribution of doctors in comparison with the population's location. A recent study by the Dartmouth Institute for Health Policy and Clinical Practice that looked at children's medical care found that there were enough pediatricians in total in the US but that over one million children live in areas without a local pediatrician.[318] In one state, Mississippi, 42% of the children

---

[318] "Many Children Lack Doctors, Study Finds," *The New York Times*, December 20, 2010.

lived in regions where there were more than 3,000 children per available pediatrician; several other states have similar poor medical coverage for children while all 50 states have areas with too many and other areas with too few pediatricians. Similar problems exist for other medical specialties.

A number of programs sponsored by state governments and the National Health Services Corporation program encourage young doctors to consider practicing rural medicine. A popular TV show in the 1990s, *Northern Exposure*, dramatized the plight of a small town in Alaska which did not have a doctor.

How Discharging Patients Sooner Brings Them Back

Like luxury resorts hospitals charge by the day. Knowing this, insurance companies and other medical cost providers have encouraged doctors to release patients from the hospital sooner. The unintended consequence of this policy is that the readmission rate has increased. In net, the cost savings from early discharge have vanished. As Dr. Harlan Krumholz a cardiologist at Yale University said, "From a societal point of view, dollars spent on health care likely increased."[319] What was a sound decision on the part of the bill payers has transmogrified into a bad medical decision.

Heart failure patients, for example, spent 8.6 days in the hospital in 1993-94 but just 6.4 days in 2005-06. No doubt, reducing day's patients stay in the hospital by 25% saves money. However, over the same time span the rate of readmission to the hospital within thirty days of discharge

---

[319] Ron Winslow, "The Revolving Door at the Hospital," *The Wall Street Journal*, June 2, 2010.

increased from approximately 17% to 20%.[320] Perhaps the argument here is that making decisions based solely on dollars and cents is less likely to be efficacious, an unintended consequence, then decisions made based on medical science.

How the Medical Gate Keeper is like a Lighthouse Keeper[321]

A near vanishing job in the US is lighthouse keeper. Technological developments such as GPS navigation and improved charts (which are easily read on an iPad) have made lighthouse keepers nearly obsolete. Primary care physicians (PCPs), the gatekeepers in the American medical system, are also a disappearing breed. Unlike the rational decline in lighthouse keeper jobs, the decrease in the number of newly minted physicians choosing primary care as their field of specialization is declining because of misguided medical reimbursement policies.

An obscure organization, the Relative Value Scale Update Committee (RUC), indirectly sets the fee structure for all doctors in America. The RUC is comprised of 29 doctors who meet three times a year in order to provide The Centers for Medicare and Medicaid Services with suggested medical reimbursement fees. [322] Not all of their recommendations are accepted but most are giving the RUC enormous power over how much money doctors make. Their decisions are based on data, often out of date, about how medical work is

---

[320] Ibid.

[321] This section is similar to the earlier one, "How Rules Rule," in Chapter 6. It was important to include it in this section on the medical industry.

[322] Anna Wilde Mathews and Tom McGinty, "Physician Panel Prescribes the Fees Paid by Medicare," *The Wall Street Journal*, October 27, 2010.

performed.[323] The current set of RUC recommendations emphasizes paying more when doctors do something rather than rewarding doctors who prevent the need for further medical care. There are winners and losers in this sweepstakes. The big winners are dermatologists who are rewarded at a rate of approximately $214 per hour and the big losers are primary care physicians paid at $101 per hour.

One irrefutable truth is that people listen to incentives.[324] The failure to consider this truth has created an unintended consequence in medical schools regarding the specialties chosen by young doctors. The truthfulness of the power of incentives has been proven in countries operating under a communist philosophy (people don't work if they aren't getting the fruits of their labor), when students are paid for going to school (truancy declines), and when governments subsidize the production of something like ethanol. Young medical students are no different: they follow their elder's signals when choosing a specialty for their career. The unintended consequence of the RUC providing the government with guidelines for compensation and reimbursement is that too few physicians are choosing primary care medicine.

Apparently the RUC views the gatekeeping function of primary care physicians as less important than the services of doctors performing procedures and surgeries. The unintended consequence is that there aren't enough gatekeepers and as a consequence the system is failing. A good analogy occurred in football. Head coaches were underpaid relative to their star performers (not many coaches could sprint down the field). Football unlike medicine has most of its decisions made by the private sector and not by the government. Teams soon learned the

---

[323] Ibid.

[324] Ayn Rand said it best, "the profit motive, speaking broadly, means a man's incentive to work in order to gain something for himself - in economic terms, to make money."

importance of head coaches. College coaches now regularly make in excess of $2 million a year. Nick Sabin at Alabama earns in excess of $6 million while head coach salaries in the NFL reach as high as $8 million a year (Mike Holmgren Seattle Seahawks). A football team can't succeed without a good head coach; neither can medicine work without PCPs. Someone needs to man the gates and that someone needs to be fairly paid.

How the Medical Gate Keeper is like a Lighthouse Keeper: Part 2

What happens when the medical establishment has an insufficient number of gatekeepers? The world of tomorrow is here today, at least in Boston. According to the *Boston Globe*, it has become virtually impossible to get a new PCP at one of the city's best teaching hospitals. [325] The unintended consequence described in the section above caused by the RUC influencing the choices specialties by young doctors is not the only source of this critical shortage. An additional unintended consequence affecting the ability of patients to have a PCP is caused by the increased percentage of young doctors who are women; medical schools today have greater than 50% women in attendance. The *Boston Globe* uncovered the fact that female primary care physicians choose to work fewer hours, thereby compounding the shortage, as they choose to spend more time with their families.

Everything has an unintended consequence. Nothing escapes the power of unintended consequences to make things work out differently than we expect.

---

[325] Liz Kowalczyk, "Hospital Doctors Shut Doors to New Patients; Many are Forced to Go to Health Centers," *Boston Globe*, November 12, 2006.

Chapter 8

Distinguishing Between Unintended Consequences and Externalities

Externalities are a regular topic discussed by economists and policy analysts. Externalities are similar to unintended consequences but they are not the same thing. When parties engage in either production or consumption (let us refer to these as economic transactions) externalities may emerge and as a result a third party, not directly involved in the transaction, receives positive or negative benefits (i.e., externalities). Critical to this definition is the fact that the third party who receives the externality has no control over the transaction. For that reason, economists say that externalities cause potential misallocations of resources because the person that receives the externality's cost or benefit is not a participant in its decision process.

The classic example of a *negative* externality occurs when a company brewing beer besides a river suffers damage from another party's decision to build a polluting factory upstream from the brewery. A *positive* externality occurs if the new factory is actually hyper-green and it replaces an older factory which was a major polluter. In neither case was the brewery's owner consulted or allowed to change the development plan; in the first case, the brewery suffers a loss while in the second case it receives a gain. Both are externalities. They also are unintended consequences.

Externalities are a type of unintended consequence but all unintended consequences are not externalities. Two characteristics distinguish externalities from unintended consequences. The first is that externalities derive from economic transactions while unintended consequences result from economic transactions and from noneconomic decisions. The second is that externalities are somewhat predictable while unintended consequences (at least those that are not externalities) are unpredictable. Another way to think about this is that some externalities are not unexpected while unintended consequences are always unexpected by the primary decision-maker.

Economic transactions involve at least two parties, usually a buyer and a seller. Parties to a transaction are expected to review the terms of a deal and only proceed if they find it to be advantageous to them. A contract, written or oral, defining the bargain binds the parties to the agreement. If a party to the transaction is later unhappy with its outcome they can rely on the contract's terms for relief. Dissatisfaction with an outcome of an economic transaction is not an externality. It merely indicates that one party did not strike a good bargain for itself. Externalities only affect those not given the opportunity to influence the form or substance of a transaction. Externalities happen to third parties while unintended consequences affect both the parties to an economic transaction as well as those not involved in the transaction.

There are two types of unintended consequences. One type of unintended consequence is externalities caused by economic transactions. A second type of unintended consequence derives from any decision made by individuals, businesses or governments. Examples of unintended consequences that are not economic transactions include someone falling in love with someone new because their steady date was detained by a rainstorm; a person driving without sunglasses and having an auto accident; or even someone becoming a famous movie star because a director or producer turned their head and happened to notice the future star working at the soda fountain. Unintended consequences from non-economic transactions involving businesses include a store's awning knocking a passing bicycle rider off his bike causing injury; or a company that bans birthday parties at work finds that it suffers from a higher rate of unplanned separations. Unintended consequences not from economic transactions involving government include a decision to add another Federal holiday and celebrating workers get drunk and have accidents; or the imposition of a tax on high-income hedge fund managers that leads them to move to lower-tax countries.

The second distinction between externalities and unintended consequences is that it is easier to predict, or attempt to predict, externalities from economic transactions. Predictability derives from causality and suggests that with sufficient information an informed prediction is possible. Individuals make predictions by observing patterns of repeated behavior. For example, expectations are the rationale relied on by a landlord to refuse to rent to 10 unrelated people under the age of 21. In this case, the landlord predicts or expects the young tenants to be discourteous, loud, and prone to late nights. If the landlord's expectations are accurate, neighboring houses avoid the externality of late night parties. Landlords avoid the externality of unbearable tenants by predicting behavior and being selective in their choice of tenants.

Economic transactions whose externalities are more easily predicted involve often repeated exchanges. For example, a tannery that produces leather might be expected to discharge deadly arsenic as a byproduct of its operations. This is not the first tannery in the world so it would not be unreasonable to predict the possibility of an arsenic problem. Similarly, the consumption of hot dogs by patrons leaving a baseball game might lead to a substantial littering problem if patrons throw away the wax paper wrapper and the paper tray holding the hot dog as they leave the park. This is not the first baseball park and this is not the first time hot dogs wrapped in wax paper are sold on paper trays. Damage to the surrounding community from hot dog vending is predictable. In contrast, externalities from infrequent or new economic transactions are harder to predict. For example, recently scientists reported creating the first synthetic cell. What this development may do to other cells or human life itself is unknown.

The unintended consequence, mentioned above, of someone falling in love with someone new because their steady date was detained by a rainstorm is less predictable than are externalities. Obviously this is not the first rainstorm; nor is this the first couple which had a mix up leading to a delayed date which might seem to imply that the event is predictable. However, the event is unpredictable because this is the first storm that interfered with that couple at the same time as the new person crossed paths with a member of the original couple. The inability to predict unintended consequences - love in this case - comes from a lack of clear causality between the rain storm and the new love affair and from the complexity of the facts – many other people walked by the stranded lover, the duration and severity of the storm was unknowable, whether the other driver would be delayed was uncertain, and the stranded lover's change in mood was capricious. Moreover, predictability may not be achieved because other than the person who lost their date, no one may care about this unintended consequence. In fact, the person who lost a date because of lateness may subsequently also have met someone new. That person may in fact now be happy that the unintended consequence occurred. No matter how much one cares, it is impossible to stop an unintended consequence that you can't predict, accurately time, or know where it will occur.

While it might seem reasonable to conclude that externalities are more costly and hence more important than unintended consequences because they arise from economic transactions that would not be true. In Ray Bradbury's 1952 short story *A Sound of Thunder* a time traveler accidentally steps upon a butterfly in the distant past changing the future. Brutality and repression become the norm and beauty and art are unknown. This has become known as the butterfly effect and helped to popularize the idea of chaos theory. Though the example is fictional its message resonates. Unintended consequences can create major economic and personal consequences despite the fact that they may originate from a noneconomic event or transaction. Take for example the assassination of Archduke Franz Ferdinand of Austria in 1914, an event that led to World War I and which cost millions of innocent people their lives and freedom. The assassins hoped to force the Austro Hungarian Empire to split off a piece of itself into a Greater Serbia. Worldwide monetary and nonmonetary impacts that resulted from the unintended consequences of the Archduke Ferdinand's assassination were astronomical. The cost of these unintended consequences may outweigh the sum of the cost of all externalities caused by every economic transaction between the war years, 1914 – 1918.

Ronald Coase, the winner of the 1991 Nobel Prize in Economics, is known in part for his 1960 paper entitled "The Problem of Social Cost" in which he argued that externalities are resolvable by improving the way property rights are defined. He felt that two neighboring businesses whose interest's conflict would seek to resolve an externality by the business which generated the most profit paying the other business to not interfere with them. For example, if the brewery were highly profitable while the polluting upstream factory was not, the brewer might pay the other factory not to operate or to clean up its operations. Coase was not writing about unintended consequences. A better property rights system would do little to minimize the cost of unintended consequences that were not based on economic transactions. Something beyond Coase's idea is needed. This starts with gaining a fuller understanding of the social ramifications and the personal consequences of unintended consequences so that their negative impacts can be reduced.

Externalities affect secondary and tertiary parties to an economic transaction. While it is difficult to trace parties affected by externalities with existing legal contracts they can often be identified by simply following reasonable deductive patterns. For example, in the brewery example above, as soon as the new plant is announced, the brewery's owners can predict that their operations will be affected by this plant decision. Everyone knows that the new factory's operations will affect the water's purity, that water moves downstream, and that the brewery is located down river from the new factory. If society cares enough about externalities, it could regulate economic transactions and permit externalities to be part of the decision making process. Currently, we don't follow this approach and instead we resolve externalities post event in the court of law. BP p.l.c. is destined to a multi decade sojourn in numerous courts as it works to resolve lawsuits arising from the Deepwater Horizon oil rig explosion and leak offshore Louisiana. In contrast, it is not possible to predict the unintended consequences of someone forgetting to wear sunglasses. There are so many permutations of outcomes which themselves are affected by actions taken immediately following the person driving away without sunglasses that prediction is impractical if not impossible.

Just because externalities are predictable does not mean that our society devotes any resources to that effort. We have a hard enough time clearing the snow off of roads. Our society often fails to invoke either punishment or reward to deal with the economic ramifications of positive or negative externalities. Instead, complaints are brought to the courthouse where negative externality defendants profess their lack of responsibility for the damages, damage estimates are contentious, and cases often linger in courts for decades while litigants pursue justice; examples include the Dalkon shield litigation, multiple asbestos litigations, or even one neighbor suing another over the height of a fence or the location of a tree limb. Regarding positive externalities, there is little support for the notion that the resulting gains should be shared between the party whose actions created the positive externality and the agent deriving the benefits. Yet it is "possible" for society to require parties to an economic transaction to determine who their actions affect and to try to mitigate negative consequences or to seek recompense from gains.

Predictability matters. Society could minimize externalities if it wanted to. To do so the unintentional impacts of economic decisions would be subjected to analysis and quantification. Unintended consequences are harder to trace (would sunglasses have prevented the accident), causation is difficult to prove (was the sun out at the precise moment of the accident), and affected parties may be far removed in time and space. Finally, unintended consequences are often more subtle in their impact than are externalities.

This realization is this book's thesis. Efforts to limit unintended consequences should only apply to government decisions. Decisions made by individuals have a limited range both spatially and in terms of the number of individuals affected. They spread within a very small circle. In contrast, government decisions have the most widespread geographical and personal impact and their unintended consequences impact the greatest number of individuals. Not only that but if the negative effects of unintended consequences are linear than decisions made by people cause a limited amount of damage while those made by government create the most damage.

Damages from company induced unintended consequences are probably more costly that those caused by individuals but less costly than those from government. Our society has fewer regulations on people or government than on companies. Nothing forestalls an individual from buying a surplus army tank; similarly, there is little stopping government from imposing unpopular laws like The Patient Protection and Affordable Care Act (ObamaCare). In contrast, companies are regulated by innumerable agencies including the Food and Drug Administration, the Federal Aviation Administration, the Occupational Safety and Health Administration and on and on. [326] There actually exists something called The Code of Federal Regulations (sometimes called Administrative Law) which in its 50 volumes contains all the rules and regulations enacted by just the federal government. State laws add to this list of control over companies. All these constraints on companies,

---

[326] The cost of regulation imposed on all business by the Federal government was estimated for the year 2008 as $1.75 trillion by Nicole V Crane and W Mark Crane, *The Wall Street Journal*, September 27, 2010.

keep their unintended consequences less harmful than those caused by an unfettered government.

      I would like to end this chapter and this book with a quote from Will Rogers, the famous American humorist from the 1920s and 1930s. In 1930 Rogers wrote in *The New York Times*, "this country has come to feel the same when Congress is in session as we do when the baby gets hold of a hammer. It's just a question of how much damage he can do with it before you can take it away from him."[327] The same can be said today. Despite their best efforts, our Congressional leaders generally leave behind a legacy of poorly enacted laws and regulations. Granted some of these pieces of legislation in terms of their initial impacts on society yielded positive benefits but when the calculus includes the secondary and later effects of legislation, after the onset of unintended consequences, the overall impact on society is often negative.

---

[327] See, Jeff Sommer, "If Congress Stalls, Do Stocks Rise?, *The New York Times*, September 26, 2010, page BU5.

www.ingramcontent.com/pod-product-compliance
Lightning Source LLC
Chambersburg PA
CBHW060845280326
41934CB00007B/923